AN INTERDISCIPLINARY APPROACH
TO MULTICULTURAL TEACHING
AND LEARNING

AN INTERDISCIPLINARY APPROACH
TO MULTICULTURAL TEACHING
AND LEARNING

Edited by

Emma Thomas Pitts

and

Rose M. Duhon-Sells

Mellen Studies in Education
Volume 24

The Edwin Mellen Press
Lewiston/Queenston/Lampeter

Library of Congress Cataloging-in-Publication Data

An interdisciplinary approach to multicultural teaching and learning /
edited by Rose M. Duhon-Sells and Emma Thomas Pitts.
    p.   cm. -- (Mellen studies in education ; v. 24)
    Includes bibliographical references (p.....).
    ISBN 0-7734-8839-1 (hard)
    1. Multicultural education--United States. 2. Interdisciplinary
approach in education--United States. 3. Activity programs in
education--United States. I. Duhon-Sells, Rose M. II. Pitts, Emma
Thomas. III. Series: Mellen studies in education ; v. 24.
LC1099.3.I477 1996
370.19'6--dc20   95-41002
                                                              CIP

This is volume 24 in the continuing series
Mellen Studies in Education
Volume 24 ISBN 0-7734-8839-1
MSE Series ISBN 0-88946-935-0

A CIP catalog record for this book is available from the British Library.

The Edwin Mellen Press   The Edwin Mellen Press
        Box 450   Box 67
    Lewiston, New York   Queenston, Ontario
    USA 14092-0450   CANADA L0S 1L0

The Edwin Mellen Press, Ltd.
Lampeter, Dyfed, Wales
UNITED KINGDOM SA48 7DY

Printed in the United States of America

TABLE OF CONTENTS

ACKNOWLEDGEMENTS

So many people set aside their personal schedules to participate in a Summer Institute to understand and subsequently better the conditions of others. To them through their untiring efforts and commitments to the cause, we say "thank you."

The authors are deeply indebted to all of the participants of the Institute of Multicultural Education which was recently held on the Southern University Campus. The consultants, presenters, parents, teachers, and students were enthusiastic, concerned, and willing to "attack" the subject of multicultural education. They expressed many positive comments about the need for understanding in our culturally-diversed society. It is the recommendation of this group that data will be collected continuously and that other such public forums will address the needs of the culturally different in the classroom.

The multicultural education thrust should be implemented so that teachers can learn to utilize the unique cultural assets of their students in creating a learning environment that will be beneficial to all students regardless of their background.

i

INTRODUCTION

Many students in today's classrooms feel threatened by the subject matter itself and other students who seem to be "different" in their immediate environment--the classroom. They have not had the opportunity to experience the pleasure of exploring, experimenting, and sharing ideas at a level which would become an incentive to create an interest or desire for further learning.

An Institute on Multicultural Education was developed and implemented at Southern University. It was designed to develop a positive, appealing atmosphere that helped teachers, parents, and students collaborate in the process of making subjects such as math, science, history, and language a forum for learning about themselves and culturally different groups while experimenting and exploring scientific, mathematical, historical, and language aspects of their immediate environments. The project also helped teachers at the elementary and secondary levels to identify teaching strategies that will create an incentive for learning in all students and especially those who are at-risk of school failure, early dropout or becoming a victim of abuse. Training sessions were designed around four primary goals:

(1) provided a forum from which teachers, parents, and students collaborated in the experimentation and exploration of their respective teaching and/or learning areas; (2) identified teaching strategies that created an incentive for learning within elementary and secondary schools; (3) ensured that the program was assessed and monitored as a research study to offer other teachers; and (4) incorporated within the training design, teachers, parents, students, and consultants/lecturers from a diversity of pertinent local resources in order to effect a holistic approach to the study of math, science, history, and language subjects.

Accomplishment of the aforementioned goals were facilitated by the recruitment of 16 classroom teachers in the areas of math, science, history, and language from five Southeastern Louisiana parishes and the state of Florida. To effect coordination with existing programs designed to attract learners considered "at risk," 14 students were recruited through an University's Summer Program targeted to reach "at risk" students.

A cornerstone to the infusion of multicultural learning styles in any subject is an understanding of the needs of minority learners. Participants responded positively to classroom projects, activities, community-based learning experiences, and the construction of word problems from terminology present with the students' culture or home/community. The purpose of this book is to share some of those activities, resources within the community, terminology, and other classroom projects that were used in the Institute to further the learning and teaching of all classroom teachers and students in the future.

The multicultural education thrust should be implemented so that teachers can learn to utilize the unique cultural assets of their students in creating a learning environment that will be beneficial to all students regardless of their background.

CHAPTER 1

FACTS ABOUT AIDS

By: Rosa Lee Brown

INTRODUCTION

This chapter focuses on the facts about AIDS and its effect and impact on individuals. AIDS is a growing disease not only in America but all over the world. It has affected the lives of people of many diversed cultures. Many eyes and minds were closed about this disease until Earvin "Magic" Johnson opened our eyes and minds, announcing that he was infected by the HIV virus. Many individuals heard this dreadful news and began to think that anyone could get this serious disease and how it may impact lives.

AIDS stands for Acquired Immune Deficiency Syndrome. This disease affects the white blood cells which protect us from such things as the common cold. With this disease the common cold can become a deadly virus that leads to the flu and pneumonia. But, before you get AIDS you go through two other stages; ARC (AIDS Related Complex) and HIV (Human Immodeficiency Virus). ARC is the second stage of the virus. This occurs when the infected individual experiences repeated infections, swollen lymph glands, fever, nausea, and a sore throat. HIV is the first stage of the virus. You can go at least ten (10) years without knowing that you are infected. This is one of the main reasons that people should take the tests available for the virus.

The two most common ways known to get the AIDS virus are through sexual contact and blood transfusions. What is known about the transmittal of the disease is that male homosexuals, drug addicts who inject drugs, and hemophiliacs who receive blood transfusions all are high-risk groups. Some medical authorities claim that you cannot get the virus from hugging or kissing a person infected with the virus.

Treatments to counter the effects of AIDS may involve the use of antibiotics, surgery to remove skin cancer, chemotherapy, and drugs to raise the body's resistance to the disease. No cure for the disease itself has been yet found. There are no specific means of preventing AIDS.

This chapter serves to enhance the student's knowledge of AIDS and to help the student understand the impact and effects this dreadful disease has on its victims. Students must become aware that AIDS is increasingly affecting more of the general population, especially the sexual partners and children of its victims. Students must realize that anyone can get AIDS, even you!

PURPOSE SETTING QUESTIONS

1. What is acquired immune deficiency syndrome?
2. Which groups of individuals are in the high risk category for contracting the virus?
3. Why should people take advantage of the available tests for the virus?
4. AIDS stands for _____?
5. If ARC is the second stage of the AIDS virus, what is the first stage? Explain.

6. How long may an individual be infected without knowing it?

7. Which blood cells does the virus affect?

8. Can an individual become infected with the AIDS virus by kissing an infected person? Explain in full.

9. Explain the difference between HIV and full blown AIDS.

10. What are the known treatments for the AIDS virus?

VOCABULARY

TECHNICAL TERMS	COMMON TERMS
Associates	Friends
Dash	Run
Instructing	Teaching
Clan	Family
Career	Job
Saunter	Walk
Communicating	Talking
Illness	Disease
Market	Store
Comprehend	Understand
Conference	Meeting
Embrace	Hug
Spokesman	Speaker
Gathering	Group
Photograph	Picture

SPECIAL PROJECTS

(Out-of-Class Activities)

1. Students will do a research project on the HIV virus and point out the difference between the HIV virus and the full blown AIDS virus. Each paper should include the causes of AIDS, its impact on the black community, and the high risk groups affected by the virus.

2. Students will visit a local health facility to study the precautions and care used in the treatment of AIDS patients.

3. Students will write to the World Wide Health Organization in Washington, D.C. to receive information on the spread of AIDS throughout the world. Contact Health ministers of Kenya and Nigeria to find out the precautions they are using to combat the spread of the virus. This information is to be compiled and compared with several other countries including the U.S.

4. Students will visit the library using library references, vertical files, newspapers, and medical journals to find out the number of AIDS patients in Louisiana.

5. Students will visit a local hospital to interview at least two AIDS patients.

Motivational and Creative Activities

1. Students will interview peers on their feelings about the AIDS virus and construct a databank on information gathered.

2. Students will perform a skit depicting how they would treat an AIDS infected student.

3. Students will view a filmstrip on the AIDS virus and its impact on the victim and write an essay on information gained from the film.

4. Students will have a formal debate on the issues surrounding the HIV virus. They will also debate the causes of the virus and its impact on the victims.

5. Students will do a demonstration on how viruses such as AIDS can be spread. A group of five (5) students will be responsible for making up an activity using candy.

RESOURCE PLACES IN THE COMMUNITY

1. East Baton Rouge Parish Library
   7711 Goodwood Boulevard
   Baton Rouge, LA   (504) 389-3370

2. Louisiana State Department of Health
   1201 Capitol Access Road
   Baton Rouge, LA   (504) 342-9500

3. Earl K. Long Memorial Hospital
   5825 Airline Highway
   Baton Rouge, LA   (504) 356-3361

4. Hospice Foundation of Greater Baton Rouge
   3765 Government Street
   Baton Rouge, LA   (504) 343-8833

5. Louisiana State University
   Medical Research Department
   LSU Campus
   Baton Rouge, LA   (504) 383-1686

CHAPTER 2
ALGEBRIAC THINKING

By: Reginald Collins

INTRODUCTION

Algebra is sometimes spoken as the shorthand of computation. It is generalized arithmetic. Algebra enables a person to think mathematically without being confined to figures. With it, the more advanced arithmetic becomes easier. It uses letters as well as figures for members. It uses the rules of arithmetic, and some more on its own. Algebra uses an additional way to solve problems; it uses equations. The name of this branch of mathematics, the importance of equations for the word Algebra from which it is derived probably means the science of equations.

Algebra developed along with arithmetic. The algebraic way of thinking had its beginning in Babylonia and Egypt, but what is not taught in Algebra is not so old. It began in the sixteenth and seventeenth centuries and has grown in scope and uses.

Algebra and geometry are very important in the sciences and in the application of the sciences to our industries. These subjects provide training in

8

ways of thinking as well as in skills in computation. Some students who want to become experts in certain kinds of work should study even more advanced mathematics. In many schools work in Algebra begins in the eighth grade, but the regular course is given one or two years later. A second course which is an extension of the first may follow in the eleventh or twelfth grade. What is learned in Algebra is used in geometry, trigonometry, and calculus. In fact, training in algebra is required for all later work in mathematics.

In the first course of Algebra one usually learns to use a little of the "shorthand;" that is, to use letters in addition to figures to represent numbers. Sometimes these are the initial letters of words such as "t" for time, "r" for rate, "d" for distance, "i" for interest, "b" for base, "a" for altitude, "c" for circumference, "p" for principal, and "a" for area. One learns also that $N+4$ means a number increased by 4, N-4 means a number decreased by 4, 4n a number multiplied by 4, and 1/4n or N/4, a number divided by 4. Then one learns better how to read in word formulas that are expressed with letters.

PURPOSE SETTING QUESTIONS

1. Evaluating mathematical expression involves what five steps?
2. To solve an equation what do you do?
3. When adding or subtracting equations, what steps are needed to follow?
4. Why do equivalent equations have the same solutions?
5. What steps are involved when solving equations involving two operations?
6. How can you use a formula as a short way to state a rule?
7. With an inverse operation, the final result is what?

8. Multiplication signs are usually omitted before variables or an expression in parenthesis. Why shouldn't you omit the multiplication sign between two numbers?

9. Ellen has 4 less than 3 times as many stamps as George. Ellen has 92 stamps. Use this information to find out how many stamps George has.

10. Angela has a part-time job that pays $3 per hour. She wants to earn $73. How many hours must Angela work to earn the money?

VOCABULARY

TECHNICAL TERMS	COMMON TERMS
Reciprocal	Mutual
Variable	Changeable
Element	Constituent
Equal	Equivalent
Constant	Steady
Base	Foundation
Property	Money
Number	Unit
Rational	Reasonable
Theory	Explanation
Principal	Paramount
Whole	Total
Absolute	Entirety
Real	Actual
Opposite	Reverse

SPECIAL PROJECTS
(Out-of-Class Activities)

1. Visit a car dealership and find out the amount of money a dealer pays a factory for a car (dealer's cost). To make a profit a dealer must charge a customer more than the dealer's cost. Observe the price of the car along with the listed amenities on the window. Record findings.

2. Consult several consumer magazines and compare prices on different models, make, and year of cars. Use algebraic formulas to determine which car will be the most economic and wise buy for you.

3. On the average, families should expect to pay about 25 percent of income for housing costs. Visit several housing complexes and compare the prices of apartments based on geographic location, aesthetic enhancements, and your take home pay. Make notes of all observations.

4. Visit a University athletic department. Secure statistics on the attendance record increase and decrease in number of persons in attendance for the last five years.

5. Many hospitals, health insurance companies and health equipment manufacturers require the service of medical record administrators. Visit a local hospital and do the following: Describe the medical record department and compile the following statistics on the number of male and female surgery patients over a three-year period.

Motivational and Creative Activities

1. A department store sells TVs from 5 different manufacturers. Each manufacturer offers a choice of screen in 8 different sizes. All TVs are available in either color or black and white. If one TV is chosen at

random as a prize in a contest, what is the probability that it will be a Brand X color TV in the largest size available?

2. Secure a copy of an income tax general instructions form and solve this problem. Bert Steiger is a single 18-year-old student. Last year he worked for both the Valley Supermarket, where he earned $1511.72, and the Ace Construction Company, where he earned $1396.26. What was his gross income for the year? Is he required to file a tax return?

3. The cash value of a policy is the cash amount available to the insured if he or she were to surrender the policy or to borrow against the policy. Using a table provided, solve the following problem: Jason Williams is 20 years old. He wants to buy $25,000 worth of straight life insurance. What is the total amount he will pay in premiums in 15 years? What will be the cash value of his policy at the end of 15 years?

4. A clothing manufacturer makes dresses in 10 styles. Each style is made in 4 different colors and 6 sizes. A different code number is used for each style-color-size combination. How many code numbers are there?

5. Barbara has 8 mystery books, 6 science fiction books, and 5 animal books. She wants to take one of each on a camping trip. From how many combinations can Barbara choose?

RESOURCE PLACES IN THE COMMUNITY

1. Woodfin-Smith
   300 Wooddale Boulevard
   Baton Rouge, LA   (504) 926-7171

2. Athletic Department
   Southern University
   Baton Rouge, LA   (504) 771-3170

3. Baton Rouge General Health Center
   8585 Picardy Avenue
   Baton Rouge, LA   (504) 763-4000

4. Terrebonne Reading Center
   112 Colyell Street
   Houma, LA   (504) 851-3613

5. Sylvan Learning Center
   1 Oak Square
   Houma, LA   (504) 873-7323

CHAPTER 3

ENERGY

By: Alma Corbett

INTRODUCTION

This chapter is an introduction to the concept of energy. It examines or tells of various forms of energy. All around us matter is moving. For example, airplanes. You can see the planes moving but not the air, yet the air is moving, too.

Whenever matter moves, work is being done. We must have energy. It is the ability or the know-how to do work.

Another thing that is important is that it also takes energy to make matter change. Matter can change from one thing into another. For example, water can change into ice and wood can change into ashes if it is burned.

There are many forms of energy. Various energy forms include heat, light, sound, electric, stored, and motion energy.

First of all, heat energy can change matter from one state to another. Heat energy makes bits of matter move. For example, watch water heating in a pot.

As the water gets hotter, it moves around more. Of course, as the bits of matter that make up water get more energy, they move faster. Another example would be a Hershey candy bar, which, when heated, changes into liquid chocolate.

Heat energy: Can we do without it? I am sure we can't. We use heat energy for many things--just to name a few: a match, the toaster, a heater cooking our food, keeping warm, ironing our clothes, starting our cars, melting ice cubes and for many other things.

Another form of energy is light energy. Light energy is a special reaction within the sun that produces large amounts of light energy. Light energy can move from place to place without passing through matter. Light energy travels through empty space to reach earth. However, if needed to pass through matter, we would have no light from the sun or star.

If you have ever walked in the park at night, you know the importance of light energy. Without light energy, you cannot see. At night you use light energy from lamps or candles.

Light energy is used in many other ways. Plant uses it to make food. Lasers are a source of light energy that is used in surgery, especially in eye surgery and to cut through steel.

A third kind of energy is sound energy. We need energy to make sounds. Sounds are caused by things that move. Sound energy is caused by vibrations of matter. A vibration is a rapid or fast back and forth motion. The strength of the vibration that reaches the ear is determined by the loudness, which is one of the characteristics of sound. The other two are pitch and quality.

A fourth form of energy is electric energy. Electric energy takes place when the sun's energy is changed by solar cells. Objects that can change wind energy to electric energy are known as windmills. Electric energy is one of the most useful forms of energy.

Some of the electric energy people use comes from batteries, cars, flashlights, toys with batteries, running appliances, lighting homes, building, street lights, heating homes, and many, many more uses.

A fifth energy is stored energy. Another name for stored energy is chemical energy. Stored energy is released when matter is changed chemically. Much of the energy we use is stored in matter. For example, energy is stored in the food you eat, in wood, in the chemicals that are found in batteries.

A sixth form of energy is motion energy. Motion energy or kinetic energy is the energy of an object in motion. When an object stops moving, its kinetic energy changes to another form of energy, such as light, heat, or sound.

The amount of motion energy an object has depends on two things. One, how fast the object is moving and two, how much matter or mass the moving object has. Some examples of motion energy are power tools, cars, trains, motors in washing machines, drills, and rides at amusement parks.

In conclusion, we have talked about the concept of energy, while discussing and examining the many kinds and forms of energy. Also, we have learned how energy changes. We have examined several changes and identified the changes in energy form.

On the other hand, we have learned about energy sources, including fuels, moving water, wind, and solar energy. In addition, we have discovered and talked about how these sources are used by people. Identification has taken place between the relationship of work, energy and matter. We have talked about the many kinds of energy forms, including heat, light, sound, electric, stored and motion energy. We have taken heat energy and changed it into matter, while recognizing forms of stored energy.

Finally, we have described motion energy in terms of mass and speed.

PURPOSE-SETTING QUESTIONS

1. What do you think causes a fireworks display?
2. How are the rockets sent into the sky?
3. What happens when rockets explode?
4. How is matter being moved or changed by energy when airplanes are flying high in the sky?
5. How does heat energy affect the state of matter?
6. What are some examples of heat changing the state of matter?
7. What makes one sound louder than another?
8. What is used to produce your voice and make you and others talk?
9. How long does it take light to travel from the sun to the earth?
10. What are lasers and name some uses for lasers?

VOCABULARY

TECHNICAL TERMS	COMMON TERMS
Energy	Force
Laser	Light
Vibration	Tremor
Matter	Stuff
Work	Labor
Solid	Thickness
Liquid	Juice
Power	Strength
Factory	Plant
Mass	Lump
Heat	Hot
Light	Lamp
Sound	Noise
Electric	Energy
Motion	Action

SPECIAL PROJECTS

(Out-of-Class Activities)

Activity No. 1

How to Change Energy

a. Put a string through two holes in a button.

b. Tie the ends together to make a loop. Slide the button to the middle of the loop.

c. Hold each end of the logs and twirl the button 30 times.

d. Pull out on both ends of the string.

Materials Needed

1. large button

2. string

Activity No. 2

Collage on Energy

a. Collect several magazines.

b. Find pictures on energy and cut them out.

c. Use a 9 x 12 poster and glue the pictures in a pleasing arrangement.

Materials Needed:

1.	Magazines	3.	Elmer's glue
2.	Poster	4.	Scissors

Activities No. 3 and No. 4

Forms of Energy

a. Collect pictures to represent each form of energy listed.
   (light, heat, electric, stored, motion and sound)

b. Glue them on a sheet of paper and label each one.

c. Bring it to class and discuss it.

Activity No. 5

<u>Showing Energy Change</u>

a. Draw four rectangles (boxes).

b. In box 1 draw a picture of energy being used in some way.

c. Name the form of energy being used on the line in Box 2.

d. Name the form also in Box 3.

e. Show how the energy can change to another form of energy. Name the form of energy.

RESOURCE PLACES IN THE COMMUNITY

1. Barkiel Electric Incorporated
    767 Steele Boulevard
    Baton Rouge, LA   (504) 383-6791

2. Notoco Industries Incorporated
    10380 Airline Highway
    Baton Rouge, LA   (504) 292-1303

3. Quality Electric Incorporated
    9050 Tiger Bend Road
    Baton Rouge, LA   (504) 752-7344

4. Public Works Department
    444 St. Louis
    Baton Rouge, LA   (504) 389-3168

5. North Landfill
    16001 Samuels Road
    Zachary, LA   (504) 389-4813

CHAPTER 4

SPEAKING AND LISTENING

By: Debra Gipson

INTRODUCTION

This chapter is about developing skills in speaking and listening by conveying messages. In order to succeed in these skills, students must be able to articulate well and fully understand what is being said.

In this chapter, I will point out different segments of speaking, listening, speaking with body language, and a combination of speaking and listening activities.

The term "communication" is often used to include only the spoken word and its perception; however, speech and hearing comprise only one of the many aspects of communication.

Telecommunication carries its original broad meaning: To communicate at a distance. People will "reach out and touch someone" with a phone call, curl up with a good video disc, or simply turn on the local TV news; they will all be experiencing telecommunication in this sense.

It has been almost thirty years since the Ampex Corporation introduced a tape recorder capable of reproducing television industry to many electronic manufacturers that worked to develop a system for recording television images on magnetic recording tape.

Any room produces reverberation and it will exhibit one or more resonant frequencies. Room reverberation time depends upon the amount of sound energy absorption that occurs. Reverberation time is defined as the time that is required for a sound burst to decay 60 db from its initial intensity. A result of reverberation is partial cancellation of particular audio frequency and is determined chiefly by its dimensions. If the walls, floor, and ceiling of a room are acoustically reflective and in turn produce substantial echoes, the sound wavefront requires a comparatively long time to decay, and the sound energy that started from a particular location then reaches the listener from many directions.

It is recognized that the human ear is tolerant of a reasonable amount of reverberation. In fact, an anechoic room that has no reverberation sounds "unnatural" to the listener. Although a sound may reach the listener from two different directions, he/she will perceive the source of the sound as in the direction of the louder wavefront, provided only that the time delay between the arrival of the two wavefronts is less than 25 milliseconds. If this time delay is much greater, the listener then perceives two different sources for the sound. The velocity of sound in air is slightly greater than 1000 feet per second. Reverberation time can be controlled by use of various kinds of materials within the listening area. Hard materials reflect a large amount of sound energy and thereby increase the reverberation time. On the other hand, soft materials absorb a large amount of sound energy and thereby decrease the reverberation time.

The new technique used microphones to convert sound into electrical current and then amplified the current by vacuum tubes. Now the sound of a full-sized orchestra or chorus could be recorded in all its subtlety. In 1925 the first hit of the electrical recording era appeared.

It has been almost thirty years since the Ampex Corporation introduced a tape recorder capable of reproducing television industry to many electronic equipment manufacturers that work to develop a system for recording television images on magnetic recording tape.

The assorted speakers, amplifiers and turntables opposite make up only a fraction of the elaborate equipment available to the stereo buff. Each item is designed to get the most out of stereophonic sound, whether it be a symphony or the recording of racing sports cars.

PURPOSE SETTING QUESTIONS

1.   How can you develop good listening skills?

2.   What can you do to improve your articulation?

3.   What is meant by pantomine?

4.   How do speaking and listening relate to each other?

5.   If I read you a story, who would be the speaker and who would be the listener?

6.   Can you speak and listen at the same time? Why or why not?

7.   Do you learn from talking to someone? Explain.

8.   How can listening help you become a better speaker?

9.   When is it time to listen?

10. Why can't we speak clearly with our mouths closed?

VOCABULARY

TECHNICAL TERMS	COMMON TERMS
Develop	Grow
Articulate	Speak
Humorous	Funny
Gigantic	Big
Status	Position
Proposal	Plan
Territory	Land
Sparrow	Bird
Consolidate	Combine
Chamber	Room
Modify	Change
Entire	Whole
Gravitate	Move
Inflate	Swell
Unique	Different

SPECIAL PROJECTS
(Out-of-Class Activities)

1. Students will visit a local TV newsroom to see the importance of speaking fluently so that the correct message will be conveyed.

2. Students will visit the School for the Visually Impaired to fully understand that when one general organ is absent, such as sight, listening is of greater importance.

3. A trip to the telephone company can enlighten students on the importance of listening in order to obtain and relay correct messages.

4. Planning a trip to The School for the Deaf will prepare students for communicating with deaf people. This trip will show them how to speak with their hands. They will learn that body movements is very important when speaking.

5. Students will visit the Speech and Hearing Foundation to learn about the technical side of listening and sound such as acoustics.

Motivational and Creative Activities

1. Reporters (interviewing) - Students will have to do a survey about the most popular TV shows. Each student will interview an older sibling or a friend about his or her favorite TV show.

2. Read and Record (Speaking) - Each student will be assigned a selection to read into the tape recorder. Parts of the tape will be played for a class discussion.

3. Oral Talks (Speaking) - Have students prepare and give oral talks on how to do something, complete with demonstrations.

4. Time Out (Listening) - Students are to put their heads down on their arms, close their eyes, and remain totally silent for five minutes. At the end of

that time, they should list all of the things they heard. Discuss their completed lists, noting especially things that were listed that would have been unnoticed under ordinary classroom circumstances.

5.   Videotaping (Speaking/Listening) - Try to obtain the use of a video camera to record students' speeches, plays, demonstrations, and other oral presentations. Observing the tape gives students unique insight into how well they use body language, whether or not their eye contact is good, and whether they present a good appearance.

Enhancing Speaking and Listening Skills

In choral reading the students will recite together some of their favorite poems. Group letter - allows students to take turns dictating sentences for a group letter. Alliterative Sentences: Encourage clear diction and articulation as the children recite these tongue-twisting sentences. Example: Millie, Molly, and Mamie made many magical mud pies. Time Telling: Have a regularly scheduled "telling time" during which the children can tell about their personal experiences. Complete Sentences: Let students complete unfinished oral sentences such as: "I will clean my room so that... "The word "storm" makes me think of... Introductions: Let students make up a situation in which they take turns introducing each other. Example: Introduce a new student to a friend. Puppets: The students can act out everyday events or favorite activities through the puppets. Telephone: Students will make up their own telephone situations and perform their conversations for the rest of the class. News Show: Students will organize a news show. Have individual teams report on classroom or school events such as spelling bees. Word Emphasis: Write on the board some sentences in which meaning can change according to what word is emphasized. For example: Will you walk with me? Will you walk with me. Will you walk with me? Allow the students to emphasize a different word in each of the sentences. Identifying Sounds: Have students put their heads on their desk and identify the sounds they hear-such as: clapping hands, knocking, tearing paper and dropping a book. Beginning Sounds: Tell students to stand on one foot if the word you read begins like ball. If it does not, they should stand on two feet. Word Stimuli: Read a story aloud and direct the children to respond with a certain response or action each time they hear the phrase. For example, in a story with the phrase "the old man laughed, "they could respond with "ha, ha, ha." A Listening Walk: Let the students listen carefully to all the sounds around them. Listening to Music: Play a musical tape with a variety of identifiable musical instruments in it. Let students discuss the different instruments with the class. Class and Catch: This is a listening game played with a ball. Have the students form a circle around you. Throw a large playground ball up into the air and call out a child's name. That child, when he or she hears his or her name, must run into the circle and try to catch the ball before it bounces more than one time. Listen and Remember: Recite to the students an oral list of five words. Let the students listen carefully to the words and then write them down on a sheet of paper after you have presented all five words.

In summary, these exercises will help students to become good listeners and good speakers. The reason I selected these activities is that, children learn from experiencing things. If they role play the situations, they stand to gain more from the lessons.

RESOURCE PLACES IN THE COMMUNITY

1. Braud's Telephone Service
   2541 South Street
   Baker, LA   (504) 775-1929

2. Beltone Hearing Aid Service
   8149 Florida Boulevard
   Baton Rouge, LA   (504) 928-1490

3. Data Transfer Incorporated Manufacturing
   Audio and Video Tapes
   2515 Cedarcrest Avenue
   Baton Rouge, LA   (504) 926-5407

4. Associates III Hearing, Speech and
      Learning Center
   710 Colonial Drive
   Baton Rouge, LA   (504) 927-1019

5. Baton Rouge General Health Center
   8585 Picardy Avenue
   Baton Rouge, LA   (504) 763-4000

CHAPTER 5

WHAT IS LIFE?
WHY STUDY SCIENCE

BY: Cynthia M. Patterson

INTRODUCTION

There is just one reason for studying science; that is, to learn more about ourselves and the world we live in. Man is an animal. In many ways he differs but little from other animals.

Every citizen will be able to participate more effectively in our democracy if he or she can speak out and vote intelligently.

Individuals can ask questions that involve both science principles and human welfare. This chapter consists of the following concepts.

1.   Heart

2.   Blood Vessels

3.   Blood

4.   Blood Corpuscles

5.   Plasma

6.   Function of the Blood

7.   Control of Circulation

What is Life?

Life is usually easier to recognize than define. We all recognize that a dog is alive, a stone is not. What then, are the properties of the dog that distinguishes it from those of the stone?

1.   <u>The Complex Organization of Life</u>. Some stones may seem to be rather complexed with various material scattered through them. The same basic chemical principles apply to matter formed in living things do, however, have certain distinguishing characteristics: One is that the number of different elements found in living matter is considerably smaller than the number found in non-living matter.

2.   <u>The Heart.</u> The heart is located roughly in the center of the thoracic cavity. It is surrounded by a protective membrane, the pericardium. Deoxygenated blood from the body enters the right atrium. When the atrium contracts, the blood is forced through the tricuspid valve into the right ventricle.

3.   <u>Blood Vessels.</u> Blood vessels are an artery, vein, or capillary of the body. The remainder of the circulatory system of man is referred to as the systematic or body system. Even during the moments when the heart is relaxed (diastole), there is a definite pressure in the arterial system. When the heart contracts (systole), the pressure increases.

4.   <u>Blood.</u> Blood is the medium of transport in the circulatory system. Not only does the blood transport oxygen and carbon dioxide to and from the tissues and lungs, but it also transports other materials throughout the body. Blood is a liquid tissue.

5.   Blood Corpuscles. Blood corpuscles is a liquid tissue. It consists of cells (and cell fragments) suspended freely in a water medium, the plasma.

    a.   Red Blood Cells corpuscles are the most numerous of the three types.

    b.   Normal women possess about 4.5 million of these cells in each cubic millimeter of blood.

6.   Plasma. Plasma is the fluid in which all these "formed" elements are suspended in a straw-colored liquid called plasma. A variety of molecules and ions are found dissolved in the water of the plasma. They are transported by the blood from an exchange organ or reverse supply (liver, for glucose, bone) to the tissue that needs them. Plasma contains seven percent (7%) of proteins.

7.   Function of the Blood. Two major functions of the blood are:

    a.   To transport material to and from all the tissues of the body.

    b.   To defend the body against infectious disease.

    c.   Oxygen transports as much as 90 percent of the body weight of a red blood corpuscle that consist of the red pigment, hemoglobin. Hemoglobin is protein consisting of four polypeptide chains, at the center of each heme, which is an atom or ion.

8.   The Control of Circulation. This is the amount of blood pumped to the heart that increases with exercise, and that the blood supply in the capillary blood varies from time to time over wide ranges. It is not surprising that a system as important as the circulatory

system should be flexible in its operations so as to meet the changing needs of the body. The flexibility arises from a well integrated system of controls.

The Methods of Science

Gaining knowledge about the world around us involves observing with our senses. In order to gain more accurate knowledge, scientists have developed a method for studying nature. This method often involves measuring things and drawing graphs.

The Physical Basis of Life

Matter makes up both living and non-living things. Life scientists study the non-living particles that matter is made of to better understand living things. Living things also depend on a constant supply of energy. Together matter and energy are the physical bases of life.

Theories About the Origins of Life

Scientist accept that life comes only from life. Yet, the first life forms on earth must have come from non-living chemicals. Life scientists have developed theories about how life might have possibility of life existing on other planets.

Your Heart

Students should know that there is a muscle in our body which begins working seven months before we are born. It never stops, day or night until we die.

The heart is a pump. It is powerful, as it has to keep blood going around the body nonstop. The heart is in the middle of the chest. Many people think it is on the left side because the lower part is slightly over that way.

What is your heart like? It is divided into four compartments. The top two compartments are called atria; the bottom two are called ventricles. You will also see valves. Valves stop the blood from going back the way it came.

How does the heart work? The heart beats in two stages. When blood enters the atria, they squeeze tight and contract. Blood has to travel a long way from the heart to the brain.

The Heart Beat

Students need to know that the heart beats 60 to 80 times a minute. It is faster in children, about 80 to 100 times a minute. It is very fast in young babies; it slows down in old age.

Students need to know the following about the heart:

1. How many times the heart beats in a minute

2. How to administer CPR

3. How to take a pulse by how fast the heart is beating

4. The exact location of the heart in the body (chest)

5. Study sketches of the heart and body

6. Does the blood make a complete trip through both sides of the heart as it flows through the body

The Blood

This is what your heart, with muscles and valves, is concerned with. This is what arteries and veins carry around in your body.

The Make-Up of Blood

Look at a picture of blood in a test tube. The cells which are heavier are at the bottom. The pale yellow liquid above the cells is called plasma. It is made mainly of water.

What does plasma do? Its work is to carry things around the body; it is a transparent system. It carries digested and dissolved food to cells. It also takes away all the waste materials that cells do not need. Plasma contains food,

34

nutrients, and antibodies, which fight disease. Red blood cells make up 44 percent of the blood and plasma makes up 55 percent. White cells make up less than 1 percent of the blood.

Some of the most important things students would know about themselves are:

A.   Their blood type

B.   Their family members' blood type

C.   What to do if they are classified as a free bleeder

PURPOSE SETTING QUESTIONS

1.   Which arteries in the human carry deoxygenated blood?

2.   Why are valves needed in veins, but not in arteries?

3.   What substances are found in plasma but not in lymph?

4.   What are the main characteristics that distinguish living from non-living?

5.   Does a candle flame show any of the characteristics of life? Is it alive?

6.   Make a list of the terms printed in the boldface in this chapter and check the meaning in the glossary.

7.   What is a stimulus?

8.   In what ways have discoveries in science affected your life?

9.   How much blood would an adult human need to pump every minute in order to meet his oxygen needs during strenuous exercise if he had no hemoglobin?

10.   Oxygen-transport pigments are found in crustaceans but not in insects. Explain this difference.

VOCABULARY

TECHNICAL TERMS	COMMON TERMS
Cardiac	Heart
Valve	Vein
Claret	Blood
Existence	Life
Arteries	Tubes that Carry Blood
Rhythmical	Pulsating
Capillaries	Slender Hair-Like Tubes
Component	Elements
Ingestion	Swallow
Cell	Living Matter
Plasma	Water Part of the Blood
Carbon Dioxide	Colorless Gas
Carbon Monoxide	Poisonous, Colorless, Odorless Gas
Axon Dendrite	Nerve Fiber
Scientific	Using or Applying the Laws of Science

SPECIAL PROJECTS

(Out-of-Class Activities)

1. Students should visit local hospitals or nutrition centers. (School field trip.)

2. Students will write or visit different heart associations or clinics for material pertaining to the heart. Students will draw a picture of the heart and label each part.

3. Information given at the Nutrition Center will be used in the classroom and at home. Students will put together a proper meal for breakfast, lunch and dinner.

4. Students will collect frogs and dissect frog hearts and discuss all parts.

5. Students will visit libraries and check out books on science, hearts, blood, life, etc., and write a book report in full detail on a subject of their choice. (Pictures should be included).

Motivational and Creative Activities

1. Students will use a poster, colors, colored pencils, and draw a picture of a heart. Label all parts.

   a. valves   d. left ventricle
   b. right ventricle   e. muscle
   c. right atrium   f. left atrium

2. In class, students will use a stethoscope to listen at how many times their heart beats a minute.

3. Students will use a test tube, a chemical, and blood to see if the blood plasma will appear at the top.

4. Students will dissect a chicken heart and discuss step-by-step procedure, naming the different parts.

5. Students will draw a picture of a heart and the nerves that run through the heart (pacemaker). They will demonstrate (using a colored pencil) the basic rhythm that arises by impulses.

RESOURCE PLACES IN THE COMMUNITY

1.   Heart and Fitness Center
      8550 United Plaza Boulevard
      Baton Rouge, LA   (504) 922-4355

2.   American Heart Association
      5615 Corporate Boulevard
      Baton Rouge, LA   (504) 926-2726

3.   Our Lady of the Lake Regional Medical Center
          Respiratory Care Center
      5000 Hennessy Boulevard
      Baton Rouge, LA   (504) 765-8869

4.   The Nutrition Center
      3223 Sherwood Forest Boulevard
      Baton Rouge, LA   (504) 293-5240

5.   Baton Rouge Cardiology Center
      5231 Brittany Drive
      Baton Rouge, LA   (504) 769-0933

6.   East Baton Rouge Parish Main Library
      7711 Goodwood Boulevard
      Baton Rouge, LA   (504) 389-3370

CHAPTER 6

THE CIVIL WAR

BY: Dorothy I. Smith

INTRODUCTION

Of all wars, wars between people of the same country are the most tragic. Often they are the most bitter as well. Citizens fight their fellow citizens, neighbors fight their fellow neighbors, townsmen fight their fellow townsmen. Sometimes even members of the same family fight on opposite sides.

Between 1861-1865, our country was torn apart by such a war. The North and South came to blows in the Civil, called by many people, the War Between the States.

This tragic conflict grew out of conditions of economics and slavery. Different ways of living had developed in the North and in the South. Northerners earned their living by trading, shipping, and manufacturing. The people in the South depended on farming for making a living, with cotton as their most important crop. Because of these differences in ways of living, the two sections often did not agree on important issues, such as tariff and foreign trade. When issues like these came before Congress, the North and the South frequently lined up on opposite sides. Disagreements are perfectly natural in a country as large as ours, and usually it is possible to settle them fairly and peacefully. In the early 1800's the disagreement of slavery sharply split the North and the South. The North had given up slavery because its economy did not depend upon slave labor. The southern states, on the other hand, held on to slavery, because they felt thay needed slaves to work their hugh cotton crops. This disagreement over slavery might, in time, have been worked out peacefully if it had not been for the rapid expansion of our country westwardly. Disagreements between the North and the South arose over permitting slavery in the territory in the West. For some years these disagreements were settled by compromises. Finally, the arguments became so bitter that compromising was no longer possible, and our country moved steadily toward war. In this chapter we will see how the war between the two sections came about. Indeed it was a nation divided. After the Civil War began, four slave states remained loyal to the Union. The Union's resources far outnumbered those of the Confederacy's, but the South had better soldiers and generals. Abraham Lincoln was a strong and decisive leader. Jefferson Davis, president of the Confederacy, spent too much time on military details and ignored the South's other serious problems. The Civil War changed America and confirmed the federal government's authority over the states.

PURPOSE SETTING QUESTIONS

1. How did the North and the South settle their differences for many years?

2. How did the two sections move closer to war?

3. What events led directly to war between the North and the South?

4. What dispute broke out when Missouri requested admission to the Union as a state? How was the dispute settled?

5. Why was the South anxious to keep a balance between the number of slave states and free states?

6. How was the dispute over slavery in the territories settled for the time being by the Compromise of 1850?

7. At the time, most Americans had high hopes for the success of both the Compromise of 1820 and 1850. Why did the efforts to work out a permanent settlement of the slavery question fail?

8. Do you think Southerners were justified in wanting to keep their slaves?

9. How did the Kansas-Nebraska Act reopen the slavery quarrel?

10. Do you think Southerners were justified in feeling that the election of Lincoln made it necessary for them to secede from the Union?

VOCABULARY

TECHNICAL TERMS	COMMON TERMS
Chat	Talk
Vehicle	Car
Hostile	Angry
Associate	Friend
Stroll	Walk
Embrace	Hug
Instructor	Teacher
Job	Run
Slumber	Sleep
Loafers	Shoes
Photograph	Picture
Portrait	Painting
Lawn	Yard
Conference	Meeting
Clan	Family

SPECIAL PROJECTS

(Out-of-Class Activities)

1. Students will visit a plantation home. From their visit they will write an essay expressing the feelings of the slaves who lived on the plantation.

2. Students will research information about blacks who fought with the Confederates during the Civil War and present their findings to the class.

3.   Students will interview descendants of former slaves and ask what effect did the Civil War have upon their lives and of their ancestors.

4.   Students will contact the Smithsonian Institute and get information on the role of women and other minorities during the Civil War.

Motivational and Creative Activities

1.   Debate the issue of slavery as a cause of the Civil War.

2.   Open discussion on the role of blacks during the Civil War.

3.   Perform a skit depicting the black soldier who fought during the Civil War.

4.   View a film on the Civil War and gather information for an essay paper.

5.   Do a research paper on one of the abolitionists.

44

RESOURCE PLACES IN THE COMMUNITY

1. Louisiana State University
   History Department
   Baton Rouge, LA   (504) 388-8281

2. Main Library
   7711 Goodwood Boulevard
   Baton Rouge, LA   (504) 389-3370

3. Magnolia Mount Plantation House
   2161 Nicholson Drive
   Baton Rouge, LA   (504) 343-4955

4. Louisiana State Archives
   3851 Essen Lane
   Baton Rouge, LA   (504) 922-1000

5. Southern University and A&M College
   History Department
   Baton Rouge, LA   (504) 771-4500

CHAPTER 7

THE EARTH IS HOME

FACES IN THE MIRROR

By: Lisa M. Smith

INTRODUCTION

The two units I selected were "Faces in the Mirror" and "The Earth is Home" from **Adventures for Readers**, which is a seventh grade literature book. In the school where I teach, Loggers' Run Community Middle School, team instruction is practiced. Team instruction consists of one of each of the four core-curricular: Math, Science, English and Social Studies. Instructors "team-up" to teach students. Each instructor tries to incorporate concurrent lessons that highlight a selected topic. This method generally enforces what the student learns as he moves from class to class.

For this two-week lesson, our team, 7A, selects earth as a topic. I look through the literature book to find a unit or units that also deals with our topic. I decide on Unit Three: "The Earth is Home." I also select "Faces in the Mirror", because it deals with a Multicultural infusion into literature and it talks about earth in its stories.

"The Earth is Home" is a unit that consists of a collection of poems and short stories that all deal with some aspect of nature and our responsibility to preserve it. The poems and stories have themes such as: spring, animals, weather, nature can give pleasure or nature can be destructive, nature can be an adventure or nature can be a frightening or nature as a source of power (gods - mythology).

"Faces in the Mirror" is a unit that deals with the varying cultures, customs, traditions, and races. Each story deals with a different nationality. There are stories on Indians, African-Americans, Orientals, and White Americans, and in each story an interaction with nature takes place.

As each teacher constructs his/her individual lesson plans, his/her activities serve as a review for another class.

PURPOSE SETTING QUESTIONS

1. Why is it important to save "mother earth?"

2. In what ways can we work to preserve the world around us? Name at least six ways.

3. What is the Greenhouse Effect and what "affect" does it have on this planet?

4. From your readings, name at least two ways the Indians pay homage to earth (Hint: custom).

5. Why is it important to maintain the life form balance of the sea? (Hint: See "The Wild Duck's Nest")

6. In what ways does nature give us pleasure? Cite the page where the answer is found.

7. In what ways can nature be destructive? Cite the page numbers where the answers are found.

8. In Helen Keller's story, "The Two Faces of Nature," how can nature be frightening?

9. Explain the thought: Nature as a source of power (Hint: See Mythology stories).

10. Select any three poems and identify the nature theme in your own words.

VOCABULARY

TECHNICAL TERMS	COMMON TERMS
Thong	Leather Cord
Baroque	Misshapen
Tradition	Custom
Quest	Search
Lapis Lazuli	Blue Semi-Precious Stone
Hummock	Mound of Earth
Azure	Sky-Blue
Deluge	A Flood
Atmosphere	Air Around Earth
Everglades	Swamplands
Rivulet	Small Stream
Knoll	Small Hill
Islet	Small Island
Lichen	Moss-like Plant Growth
Greenhouse	Glass where Plants Grow
Sioux	An Indian
Moor	Stretch of Open Land
Chlorophyll	Green Pigment in Plants

SPECIAL PROJECTS

(Out-of-Class Activities)

The culminating activity for this unit would be in the form of an informational fair. The class would be divided into five groups (outside of class). Each group is responsible for making a comprehensive display on their groups' topic. This display should include the following: a written report, visual aides, a prepared oral presentation, a list of other reading materials on the subject, and suggestions, where applicable, to improve the present state of their topic.

1. Water Conservation - The students in this group are responsible for completely preparing their display on water conservation.

2. Greenhouse Effect - The students in this group are responsible for completely preparing their display on the greenhouse effect.

3. Soil Erosion - The students in this group are responsible for completely preparing their display on soil erosion.

4. Air Pollution - The students in this group are responsible for completely preparing their display on air pollution.

5. Recycling - The students in this group are responsible for completely preparing their display on recycling.

Motivational and Creative Activities

Once the unit has come to an end, the class will have a three-day "informational fair," which would be followed by a quiz. (The quiz would serve as bonus, but the students would not know this).

RESOURCE PLACES IN THE COMMUNITY

1. ABC Educational Supplies
   1255 S. State Road 7
   West Palm Beach, Florida   1-800-432-0213

2. Center Supply, Inc.
   1256 S. State Road 7
   West Palm Beach, Florida
                                       1-407-697-0822

3. Drago School Supply
   8205 W. 20th Avenue
   West Palm Beach, Florida   1-800-432-0690

4. Learn, Inc.
   4122 PGA Boulevard
   Palm Beach Gardens, Florida   1-407-694-1939

5. Revelations - A New Beginning
   905 N. Federal Highway
   Lake Park, Florida   1-407-842-7707

6. T.E.A.C.H. of Palm Beach County
   3915 Jog Road
   West Palm Beach, Florida   1-407-624-9020

7. T.E.A.C.H. of Jupiter, Inc.
   1695 W. Indiantown Road
   Jupiter, Florida   1-407-747-3599

8. Palm Beach County Libraries

   6135 Lake Worth Rd.   1-407-965-2525

   1000 Townhall Avenue   1-307-744-2307

   365 Tequesta Drive   1-407-746-5970

   5760 Pkeechobee Blvd.   1-407-683-2381

   8895 N. Military Trail   1-407-626-6133

   1030 Royal Palm Drive   1-407-798-0154

9. East Baton Rouge Parish Library
    7711 Goodwood Boulevard
    Baton Rouge, LA   (504) 389-3370

10. Beau Bois Day Camp & School
    520 Halfway Tree Road
    Baton Rouge, LA   (504) 766-0536

CHAPTER 8

WHY WE NEED FOOD

By: Bertha Williams

INTRODUCTION

The chapter on "Why We Need Food" consists of three lessons. Lesson One discusses the functions of six main nutrients. Lesson Two discusses the four basic food groups and the components of a well-balanced diet. Lesson Three also discusses the relationship between energy, calories, consumption, and activity levels.

The six main types of nutrients are proteins, carbohydrates, fats, water, vitamins, and minerals. Proteins are nutrients that help your body make new cells. New cells are needed in order to grow. Many proteins come from animals. Some come from plants. Sugars and starches are also known as carbohydrates. Carbohydrates are nutrients that provide the body with quick energy. Foods that come from plants contain a lot of carbohydrates. Fruits, breads, cereals, and vegetables are carbohydrates. Fats are nutrients that give your body energy to store. Fats come from foods made from plants and animals. Plant fats are called oil. Your body makes fats from all the food you eat. Body fats store energy to used when it does not get enough food. Fat helps to keep your body warm. Vitamins and minerals help your body use carbohydrates, fats, and proteins. Some minerals help build body parts. In order for your body to get the minerals and vitamins it needs, you must eat a variety of foods. Water is a nutrient that makes up over half of your body weight. Water is necessary for life functions. Water carries food, chemicals, gasses, and wastes throughout the body. Water is the most important nutrient because it plays an important role in body functions. It carries wastes from the body in feces, urine, and sweat. The body is cooled by sweat evaporation from the skin.

The components of a balanced diet depends on the health, activity, level, and age of a person. During the years of growth a person needs a diet high in carbohydrates and proteins. As a person ages, fewer carbohydrates and fats are needed. To help you eat a balanced diet food experts have formulated the balanced diet plan. The plan classifies foods into groups and tells which foods are in each group. The four main food groups are: (1) meats, (2) fruits and vegetables, (3) breads and cereals, and (4) dairy foods. You need to eat foods from each group every day to have a balanced diet.

Your body needs energy to move, grow, keep warm, and repair itself. There is energy in food that must be changed to energy you can use. First, food moves through the digestive system. From there the digested food moves into the blood stream. The blood takes the food to body cells. Once inside the cells the food changes to energy you can use.

Various foods give you different amounts of energy. This energy can be measured in units called calories. You need a certain number of calories everyday. The amount of calories needed depends on the activity level of the individual. If you eat more calories than you can use, the extra calories will be stored as body fat. The stored fat may cause you to become overweight. Being overweight can lead to health problems.

A body's energy balance is influenced by one's sex, age, health, and size. From birth to late teens, increased growth and development results in a need for more calories. Older people need fewer calories; for example, a 60-year-old may need the same number of calories as a six-year-old child.

In summary, to maintain health and fitness, it is necessary to eat a balanced diet. Eating a balanced diet will provide your body with the nutrients required for body processes.

PURPOSE SETTING QUESTIONS

1. How do proteins help your body?
2. Why are liquids an important part of a healthy diet?
3. What is a balanced diet?
4. How can you make sure you have a healthy diet?
5. Name the food group of each food: juice, beans, cereal, cheese.
6. How can a person lose weight?
7. What are the six nutrients your body needs?
8. Why are carbohydrates good for you?
9. What do you need to eat to have a balanced diet?
10. What kinds of food might be part of a diet to lose weight?

VOCABULARY

TECHNICAL TERMS	COMMON TERMS
Diet	Food
Fat	Grease
Dairy Foods	Milk, Milk Products
Activity	Movement
Plants	Vegetables
Starch	Energy
Provide	Give
Components	Parts
Carbohydrates	Sugar
Overweight	Fat
Serving	Food Amount
Expert	Trained
Classifies	Names
Exercise	Work
Function	Act

SPECIAL PROJECTS
(Out-of Class Activities)

1. Have students list favorite foods in America that originated in other countries and tell something about each.

2. Have students use food items listed in Activity 1 to plan menus to be prepared in the food lab.

3. After discussing experts in the field of nutrition, have students prepare a list of careers in the field of nutrition with educational qualifications for each.

4. Have students list their favorite junk food snack. Using a nutrition and calorie chart, have students write nutrition value and calories provided by each. Have students prepare an alternate list of nutritious snack foods and compare to junk food list.

5. Nutrient Mobile - Students will make mobiles showing the six main nutrients needed by the body. The names of the nutrients are written on foods that provide a great amount of the nutrient. For example, potatoes are high in carbohydrates, so carbohydrates will be written on a potato for the mobile.

6. Provide students with pieces of paper and food sample rich in fat, such as cooked bacon, margarine or butter, and pecans. Also give food samples that are low in fat, such as potatoes, bread, and apples. Have students rub the samples on separate pieces of paper. The presence of a persistent translucent spot is evidence of a high fat content.

7. Many students are not aware of the appearance, taste, and texture of processed soybeans. A food containing tofu may be cooked and sampled by the class. Tofu can be found in a grocery store or an Asian food store. Tell students that tofu belongs to the meat group and that it forms an important part of many Asian diets. Other unfamiliar ethnic foods may also be used.

8. Have each student bring in food labels from a box of his/her favorite cereal. The label should have the nutrient content for one dry serving and for one serving with one-half cup of whole milk. The students are to determine the fat, carbohydrate, and protein content in the half cup of milk by subtracting the nutrient content of dry cereal from the content of a serving with milk.

Students may also compare caloric content of cereals with and without sugar on them.

Motivational and Creative Activity

Nutrition Placemats: Have students design their own placemats with colorful pictures of foods from the basic four food groups.

RESOURCE PLACES IN THE COMMUNITY

1. Louisiana Cooperative Extension Services
   LSU Agricultural Center
   Baton Rouge, LA   (504) 388-4141

2. Local Co-Operative Extension Services
   (Address and Phone Numbers will vary depending on where students live.)

3. Local Health Units
   (Address and Phone Numbers will vary depending on where students live.)

4. School Nurse
   (May be contacted through local school boards in the area where student lives.)

5. Nutrition Centers
   (Throughout the United States)

CHAPTER 9

LANGUAGE FOR DAILY USE

By: Bettye Sue Harris Wilson

INTRODUCTION

The book that I chose to use is a seventh grade English textbook: **Language for Daily Use**. This book consists of units instead of chapters. Each unit consists of several language strands where the skill is first introduced, then retaught, and finally maintained as a means of ensuring mastery of all the essential oral and written means of communication needed by the students.

People spend more time communicating than they spend in any other complex activity of life. Communication serves five major purposes: To inform, to express feelings, to imagine, to influence, and to meet social expectations. Each of these purposes is reflected in a form of communication. People spend about 45 percent of their communicating time in listening, 30 percent in speaking, and only 25 percent in reading and writing.

After a long review and decision making, I chose Unit 9 to complete my assignment. Unit 9 deals with listening and speaking skills, building vocabulary, writing letters and finally, reading letters. This unit focuses on the process of communication with emphasis on listening and speaking. In the language section of the unit, the students learn some practical techniques for listening in class, conducting a formal meeting, making introductions, conducting interviews and presenting oral reports. The study skills section enhances communication as the students study synonyms and antonyms as well as use the thesaurus. In the composition section, the students study tone and write friendly and business letters. Letters by E. B. White to a group of seventh-graders comprise the literature selection. Communication is an important part of everyone's life.

PURPOSE SETTING QUESTIONS

1. Name ways in which people communicate with one another.

2. Why is communication important?

3. Is it important to communicate clearly?

4. Can you think of a book or television show where communication is important?

5. How do people from different parts of the world communicate with each other?

6. Two new students just entered our class. Ketwago is from Africa and Nikos is from Greece. What would you do to make them feel welcome and help them meet new friends?

7. Think of a situation in which an introduction would be necessary and then write the introduction.

8. Charles, after our discussion on "Interesting and Ineffective Speakers," tell me some of the characteristics that you feel each should have.

9. You've all heard the statement, "First impressions are lasting ones." Is this important when you first meet someone?

10. Adrian: After looking through <u>Roget's Thesaurus,</u> why do you think he wrote it? Is it a helpful book? Is it a waste since we already have the dictionary?

11. Does the tone of your voice have anything to do with how effective your message is to your listeners?

12. People long ago left letters and messages that are still being read today. Why was it important for them to date and sign these messages and letters?

VOCABULARY

TECHNICAL TERMS	COMMON TERMS
Recognize	Remember, Recall
Initiate	Begin, Introduce
Informal	Casual
Formal	Dressy, Orderly
Similar	Like
Receiver	Taker
Circulating	Spreading
Greeting	Welcome, Address
Directions	Angle, Viewpoint
Details	Specify, Point
Minutes	Notes
Introduction	Preface, Preamble
Motion	Movement
Opposite	Unlike

SPECIAL PROJECTS

(Out-of-Class Activities)

1. Students will start a Pen Pal Club with children from different countries and write at least four letters during the year.

2. Play Simon Says or another similar game in order to sharpen listening skills, allowing various students to take turns being the leader and giving directions.

3. Plan a field trip to the State Capitol at a time when the legislature is in session so that students can get first-hand knowledge of parliamentary procedures.

4. Students research and report their findings on the following: an historian, the sergeant-at-arms, and the parliamentarian.

5. Have students role play right and wrong ways of introducing themselves and others.

6. Allow that artistic student the opportunity of creating a cartoon showing how you introduce yourself to others.

Motivational and Creative Activities

1. Students prepare ten (10) questions to use when interviewing someone from another country or state; then interview them and give an oral report about the person interviewed.

2. Invite or take students on a field trip to the post office. Have them interview the person. Also they will get a first-hand look at what happens to letters you write before it gets to that person.

3. Have students bring in junk business letters in order to examine their greetings, closing, and general make up.

4. Write business letters requesting information about other countries, and send for free things offered to kids.

RESOURCE PLACES IN THE COMMUNITY

1. East Baton Rouge Parish Library
   7711 Goodwood Boulevard
   Baton Rouge, LA   (504) 389-3370

2. Writing Laboratory
   Southern University
   Baton Rouge, LA   (504) 771-2503

3. Louisiana State University
   LSU Campus
   Baton Rouge, LA   (504) 383-1686

4. Associates III Hearing, Speech and
     Learning Center
   710 Colonial Drive
   Baton Rouge, LA   (504) 927-1019

5. Data Transfer Incorporated Manufacturing
   Audio and Video Tapes
   2515 Cedarcrest Avenue
   Baton Rouge, LA   (504) 926-5407

CHAPTER 10

HANDWRITING AS A CLASSROOM MANAGEMENT/SELF-ESTEEM TOOL

By: Rosena Branch-Machen

INTRODUCTION

There was a time when the only "A" on little Johnny's report card was in Handwriting. Pride was taken in learning how to write correctly and neatly. It was an accepted viewpoint that handwriting was important in the careers and daily lives of individuals such as doctors, lawyers, teachers, storekeepers, judges, even housewives in writing letters, checks, notes or lists. But Handwriting as a subject has fallen on hard times; being labeled as "busy work" and a waste of time. The state buying handwriting books is considered a waste of money and they are no longer in widespread use. So many students develop poor handwriting skills because there is no modeling and they are left to write any way the choose.

Nowadays very little emphasis is placed on the correct way of sitting, holding the pencil in the right position and slanting the paper at a comfortable angle. Pens and pencils are held in every way imaginable. Students get bumps and corns on their fingers at an early age. One can observe right-handed students writing on the left side of their desks, sitting sideways with their backs not touching or against the back of the chair. Left-handed students are holding their pencils in a stabbing position.

Over my 25 years of teaching in the elementary grades, I have seen and experienced how requiring neat and proper handwriting can settle students in a quiet and productive mood; instill pride within work is displayed or comments are made about the neatness of a student's work and the ease it gives the teacher when reading and grading papers.

First graders receive a lot of attention and practice on handwriting procedures. After that the process breaks down; so much so that a new handwriting model called D'Nealian has been developed and is published by Scott Foreman to make it easier to move from manuscript writing to cursive.

The second and third graders also need a lot of practice with a continuation of some drill in the fourth and fifth grades. The teacher should begin the first day of school showing students how to correctly form the groups of letters for manuscript or cursive writing. Time should be taken to show students how simple it is to put the strokes together to form letters. Students enjoy figuring out what strokes are used for each letter. After some practice lessons, the teacher should demonstrate by using an overhead projector or ditto sheets how the students are to head, set-up their papers, and write assignments.

Here are some procedures I have used over the years that have proven to be successful for second graders and up.

1. When heading papers students should always begin at the red left margin line; students will write their name, date and subject on the second, third and fourth lines. The left side is used so that students with long names will not have a problem of running out of space. The empty space on the right can be used to write grades and notes.

2. Students must "always" write their first and last names (self-esteem, they are important). Do not abbreviate the names of the months, or subjects. Students for the most part, do not know how to spell most of the months and subjects with ease.

3. After writing the name, date, and subject, skip a line and write the name of the skill or concept; skip a line and write Practice, Extra Practice, Review, Unit Test or whatever the assignment may be, page number and number of items, skip a line write all of the directions, skip a line and begin writing sentences or paragraphs. If writing only sentences, skip a line between each sentences. This makes it easy for both students and teacher to read and notice mistakes. There is no need to skip lines for word lists such as spelling words.

> Example:
>
> Worthington Washington
>
> Language
>
> September 1996
>
> ### Nouns
>
> Practice A, p. 26, 1 - 10
>
> Underline the noun in each sentence
>
> A.   Many cars were lined up.
>
> B.   Stickers were being checked.

4. Students should not write outside either of the red margin lines, not even for numbers. They should not try to cram all of the words in a sentence on one line. The teacher should emphasize to the students that many lines are on the paper so that they can go to the next lines if needed. Also continue assignments on the back of the paper so as not to waste paper.

5. All students' papers should be set up the same way. Their work in classwork and homework tablets and special assignment notebooks should all be headed with name, date, subject, skill, concept, page number, and number of items. When there is a need to find the work to teach, reteach or review a particular skill or concept the students can easily find it by the date, subject and/or page number.

6. Instead of using a lot of ditto work, let the students write the entire Practice, Extra Practice, Review, Study Guide or Unit Test exercises. Let them keep a folder in their desks to keep unfinished work. The teacher should not be skeptical about giving long writing assignments. This gives the students practice working in a test-like mode on a daily basis. The teacher will have time to grade papers, write lesson plans, gather and read pertinent materials, set up projects and centers and do other required school tasks. Long assignments can be divided into sections and each part used as a graded work.

7. Students should write meaningful activities and exercises. Not spelling words ten times, but putting the words in alphabetical order, writing their beginning sounds, using them in creative writing or sentences for example.

This chapter serves as a means to help teachers, students, parents, and others understand the importance of good handwriting skills in school, on jobs and in everyday living. Over the years poor handwriting has caused students to get lower grades, costly mistakes in legal matters, check writing, mail delivery and very costly ones in prescription writing in the medical field. Handwriting is a most important aspect of everyday life.

PURPOSE SETTING QUESTIONS

1. What is manuscript writing?

2. What is cursive writing?

3. What are handwriting strokes?

4. What is the correct method of holding pencils, sitting and slanting paper when writing?

5. What is the difference between letter groups?

6. How can good handwriting skills promote self-esteem in students?

7. How can requiring good handwriting help teachers with classroom management?

8. What value is good handwriting to the community?

9. How can good handwriting enhance careers?

10. How can good handwriting skills contribute to success?

VOCABULARY

Technical Terms	Common Terms
Manuscript	Print
Cursive	Script
Strokes	Marks
Baseline	Bottom line
Headline	Top line
Descender line	Line below
Midline	Middle line
Full Space	Top to bottom
Half Space	Midway
Model	Style
Write	Pencraft
Calligraphy	Penmanship
Hieroglyphic	Letter
Chirography	Alphabet

SPECIAL PROJECTS

(Out-of-Class Activities)

1. Students will cut out different styles of the same letters from newspapers.

2. Students will use modeling clay to make letters.

3. Students will use the public library to find out about graphology and its use.

4. Students will make the different types of strokes out of poster board.

5. Students will study the history of each alphabet for a role-playing activity.

Motivational and Creative Activities

1. Students will collect handwriting samples from family members, friends, and neighbors to show likeness and differences.
2. Students will make a booklet showing letter groupings.
3. Students will write a special handwriting assignment using an instrument other than a pen or pencil (ex. feather, stick).
4. Students will use a filmstrip kit to make a filmstrip about handwriting.
5. Students will view film on handwriting.

RESOURCE PLACES IN THE COMMUNITY

1. Southern University
   Writing Laboratory
   Baton Rouge, LA   (504) 771-4500

2. East Baton Rouge Parish School Board
   1050 South Foster
   Baton Rouge, LA   (504) 922-5400

3. East Baton Rouge Parish Library
   7711 Goodwood Blvd.
   Baton Rouge, LA   (504) 231-3750

4. Greater King David Baptist Church
   222 Blount Road
   Baton Rouge, LA   (504) 775-2343

5. Mt. Pilgrim Baptist Church
   9700 Scenic Highway
   Baton Rouge, LA   (504) 775-2740

6. Shiloh Baptist Church
   185 Eddie Robinson Sr. Drive
   Baton Rouge, LA   (504) 343-0640

CHAPTER 11

CREATIVE WRITING: A TOOL FOR ALL TEACHERS

By: Mary Landry Roberts

INTRODUCTION

This chapter focuses on the effectiveness of creative writing. The most effective way to improve writing is to do creative writing regularly--at least three times a week. The idea is simply to write for five minutes. Creative writing: The source of the material is within the student's real or imaginative experience, and the writing is "free" in the sense that the student has chosen his own material and is of expression. Creative writing is not made simply out of words, and no amount of training in language manipulation will ever produce it. Creative writing, as a school subject, cannot be kept confined within the framework of language study, but must overflow into that large field of the student's vital interests which education is beginning more and more to explore. The student is seeking a form of expression and a style of utterance that he can recognize as the natural vehicle for what he is trying to say. All students have need of some form of expression for what they create within themselves. Writing seems to be the most readily available medium, since it employs language skills, which everyone has to have for the affairs of everyday life.

The setting for creative expression comes about not so much because of the teacher's learning but because of the teacher's understanding. The student must feel that the teachers would know a good thing if they saw it, and that they would be happy for any student who happened to produce the writing. The students must feel confident about their creative writing and know that they would not be criticized at any point during creative writing. The teacher will maintain the students' confidence by allowing them to discover now and again that the teacher is working, even as they are working.

When the invitation to do creative writing is given on any level, the response is in terms of the individual differences represented in the class. The primary object in creative writing is to get something produced.

There are several ways of making experiences available to the whole group, to provide impulse for writing. The teacher makes it clear that what is being sought is something to write about.

The art experiment is one to impulse students to write--perhaps a painting or a picture, to be looked at and thought about. The work chosen should be something that has character, or some other intangible features. Other arts that may be used in the art experiment are sculptures and music.

Literature may also be used for it is known to carry minds up and away to places in which the student may experience a release of his own thoughts and feelings.

In addition, other activities that can be suggested by the teacher and carried out to impulse writing are special places, special people, special objects, and unique situations.

These activities should be those that automatically provide an experience and with it the stimulation for writing. The pattern for creative writing should be "observe, think, observe," then try to express the thoughts that arose in them, or the mood or feeling it gave them. Gradually, as creative writing takes effect, the experiments become less deliberate and formal. Students begin to experiment with ideas which they have chosen themselves.

Creative writing may seem crazy but actually it makes simple sense. It helps students write more easily because words will come more easily. In a creative writing exercise, the student should not stop, go back, correct or reflect. In other words, "be careless," write only what you feel. Creative writing should not be evaluated in any way. Students will begin to carry creative writing into their regular writing.

An important reason for creative writing is that it gives an opportunity for the students' emotional and imaginative life to receive recognition and training within the school. And since it is during the school years that this training is most needed, the task of teaching creative writing becomes highly important to the success of the whole educational enterprise.

PURPOSE SETTING QUESTIONS

1. What is the most effective way to improve writing?
2. Define creative writing.
3. How long and how often should a creative writing exercise take place?
4. Why should students use creative writing?
5. Why is writing the most readily available medium for creative writing?
6. How should the student feel about the teacher during a creative writing exercise?

7. What is the primary objective of creative writing?

8. Explain some ways of making experiences available to provide the impulse to write.

9. If you are participating in a creative writing exercise, what are some things that you should not do?

10. When students are participating in a creative writing exercise, what are they seeking?

VOCABULARY

TECHNICAL TERMS	COMMON TERMS
Source	Cause
Imaginative	Original
Adequate	Satisfactory
Confined	Restrict
Expression	Saying
Enterprise	Business
Evaluate	Assess
Deliberate	Consider/think
Stimulation	Excite/stir
Intangible	Abstract/vague
Criticized	Judge
Confidence	Positiveness
Utterance	Language
Manipulation	Control
Employs	Uses

SPECIAL PROJECTS

(Out-of-Class Activities)

1. Students will go to a family gathering and complete a creative writing exercise.

2. Students will visit their favorite place and complete a creative writing exercise.

3. Students will write in their home journal on a day-by-day basis.

4. Students will listen to their favorite song and complete a creative writing exercise.

5. Students will visit their grandparents and complete a creative writing exercise.

Motivational and Creative Activities

1. Students will observe and discuss a sculpture and complete a creative writing exercise.

2. While sitting in the listening center, students will listen to some Indian/African music and complete a creative writing exercise.

3. Students will think about their first day of school and complete a creative writing exercise.

4. Students will visit the zoo and express their feelings about the animals during a creative writing exercise.

5. Students will choose a special person in their lives and tell how and why that person is special during a creative writing exercise. Then students will share with the class.

RESOURCE PLACES IN THE COMMUNITY

1. Opelousas Public Library
   249 East Grolee Street
   Opelousas, LA   (318) 948-3693

2. Lafayette Public Library
   301 West Congress Street
   Lafayette, LA   (318) 261-5775

3. Opelousas Resource Center
   1070 Creswell Lane
   Opelousas, LA   (318) 948-3657

4. Eunice Public Library
   222 Second Street
   Eunice, LA   (318) 457-4196

5. University of Southwestern Louisiana
   104 University Circle
   Lafayette, LA   (318) 482-1000

CHAPTER 12

TEACHING TOLERANCE: AN IMPERATIVE FOR SOCIETY

or

PEACEFUL COEXISTENCE: TEACHING TOLERANCE

By: Elizabeth T. Evans

Rita C. Richardson

INTRODUCTION

Tolerance and sensitivity to diversity can and must be taught and learned if peace is to be achieved in our multicultural society. This chapter focuses on the use and misuse of the tolerance. Many groups in our society encourage intolerant attitudes and behaviors by employing this term out of context; thus, breeding and condoning rejection of what is considered the cultural norm.

The word "tolerance" is often misunderstood because of its various definitions. Webster's defines the term as open minded, progressive, humane, sympathetic, accepting, and forgiving. It is also defined as radical, permissive, compromising and condoning. It does not, however, mean condoning detrimental behaviors that violate the social order or breed hate, terrorism, prejudice, or incest. Which of the definitions does a society need in order to develop a democratic citizenry which will promote acceptance, empathy, appreciation and respect of difference?

Legislation may change people's behavior but is more difficult to change people's attitudes. Attitudes can be defined as predisposition toward behavior. Attitudes are learned and can be unlearned. These are often changed as a result of traumatic experiences: however, they can be changed through education and gentle persuasion. People's attitudes and behaviors change when they accept information and become aware of the fallacy that has impacted their beliefs.

Our world is evolving into heterogenous societies. Diversity can have a positive impact on communities; however, change often results in distrust and resistance. Children should be taught at an early age and throughout their adolescence and young adulthood to be sensitive to differences, to resolve conflicts without resorting to violence and to show understanding, tolerance and acceptance of other human beings. In addition, commonalities among cultures should be emphasized.

Teaching tolerance must begin at home but educators often provide additional direction in this area. Parents constantly transmit their values to their children through modeling. In addition, parents can directly communicate and teach tolerance and heighten their children's awareness of cultural differences. Often times however, it is the teacher who will first address tolerance with the children. Teachers are role models and must reflect behaviors which embrace individual differences. Students can be taught to engage in various activities to appreciate diversity and the worth of every human being.

VOCABULARY

TECHNICAL TERMS	COMMON TERMS
Tolerance	Acceptance
Discriminate	Prejudge
Segregate	Separate
Sensitive	Easily Hurt
Awareness	Understand
Appreciate	Value
Exterminate	Destroy
Embrace	Include
Communicate	Talk
Attitude	Opinion
Empathy	Share Feelings
Culture	Group
Condone	Forgive
Prejudice	Bias
Acceptance	Approval

PURPOSE SETTING QUESTIONS

1. What are the different definitions for tolerance?
2. How can the misuse of the word "tolerance" breed injustice for various cultural groups in society?
3. How has the intolerance of historical events led to dehumanizing consequences?
4. What are common attributes shared by all cultures?

5. Who is responsible for teaching children to be tolerant?

6. How does legislation affect intolerant behaviors and attitudes?

7. What are the problems and the contributions of diverse groups in a heterogenous society?

8. Why are individuals intolerant?

9. What is needed to change attitudes and promote tolerance?

10. What are the responsibilities of parents, schools, and communities to promote tolerance and acceptance of differences?

SPECIAL PROJECTS
(Out-of-Class Activities)

1. Guided Research

   Students will research the following topics:

   A. The Magna Charta

   B. The First and/or the 18th Amendment of the Constitution

   C. The Inquisition

   D. The Education of the Handicapped Act (P.L. 94-142), The Individuals with Disabilities (IDEA) Act

   E. The Nazi Extermination of the Jews

   F. Slavery in America

   G. The Irish Catholic/Protestant Conflict

   H. Ethnic Cleansing in Bosnia

2. Community Work

   Assign students to work in the community. Involve parents and obtain suggestions as to community resources. Examples: Nursing homes, Hospitals, Centers or Special Olympics.

3. Library Assignments

Ask students to research a country and write an essay entitled: "If I lived in _____." Examples: China, Australia, Mexico, Egypt, Russia, or Argentina.

4. Interviews

Interview people from different cultures. These may include ethnic groups, racial groups, religious groups, individuals with disabilities or senior citizens.

Motivational and Creative Activities

The following are some suggested activities that can be utilized to promote tolerance of various groups in society.

1. Mediation and Compromise

Read "Romeo and Juliette" or "West Side Story." How can mediation and compromise change the ending of the story? Start a school wide United Nations Club. Train students as peer mediators to resolve conflicts as they arise.

2. Books and Videos

Read/view and discuss the following:

The Diary of Ann Frank, Forest Gump, The Color Purple, I Buried My Heart at Wounded Knee, And Then Came John, Roots, or Educating Peter.

3. Leading a Helping Hand

A student with a learning disability is mainstreamed into your classroom. He has trouble taking notes in the history class. How could you offer to help? Brainstorm possible solutions.

84

4. Solve the Dilemma

Students will be given different situations and participate in solving the problems.

Examples:

A. Ann loves to play baseball and she is good at it, but she is excluded when the boys play during recess. What can Anne do to convince the boys to let her play?

B. Juan speaks English with a different accent, and the class starts to laugh. Juan feels intimidated and refuses to participate in class. What can the teacher, the students, and Juan do to solve the problem?

5. Do Unto Others

How would you want to be treated if:

-      You had a learning disability?
-      You were Black /White/Hispanic/Oriental?
-      You came from a different country?
-      You . . .

RESOURCE PLACES IN THE COMMUNITY

1. The University Library
2. Computer Data Bases: ERIC
3. Video Rental Stores
4. Local Schools: Volunteer as a tutor in an ESL class
               Volunteer in a school where students are predominantly of a different race.
5. Churches of different denominations
6. PBS Videos, 132 Braddock Place, Alexandria, VA 22314
7. Festivals celebrating various ethnic groups
8. Local Libraries

CHAPTER 13

WRITING A COURSE SYLLABUS TO
PROMOTE COGNITIVE SUCCESS IN A
MULTICULTURAL CLASS: A PARADIGM

BY: Bernice Smith

and

Lelia H. Taylor

INTRODUCTION

An effective course syllabus is a vehicle that can facilitate the empowerment of professors in the management of instructional activities. The writers believe the benefits yielded through professors' implementation of specific guidelines will maximize their planning efforts. Thus, this chapter focuses on a brief description of the rationale for including a core concept, relevant course information, course objectives, readings, descriptions of instructional procedures, and the course requirements as an integral part of a syllabus.

The Core Concept. The first section of a syllabus should necessarily be a statement of the "Core concept of the course." Students often see only topics that are listed in a course outline rather than a total image of relationships that communicate a central idea. Additionally, some students may perceive a relationship among the topics, but the image may be quite different from the teacher's, thus inhibiting their successful completion of the course. Placing a statement of the core concept of the course at the beginning of the syllabus clearly articulates the teacher's focus to the student, and facilities his formulation of a total accurate picture rather than a fragmented view of the course.

Relevant Information about the Course. The logistics of a course must be communicated to the student. He must know the course title and number to effectively evaluate the role of a given course in his curriculum. The student must know the section number, meeting days, times, and location of the course. This section of the syllabus should also provide the student with the university catalogue description of the course, the credit hours, the pre-requisites, if there are any, and the intended clientele for whom the instruction was designed. Finally, the student must be able to interact with the instructor when class is not in session, so the teacher should include his name, office hours, office telephone, electronic mail address, and fax number. When provided with essential data relevant to the course, the student is able to make intelligent curriculum decisions.

Course Objectives. Each academic discipline must choose the minimum competencies that it expects each student to have mastered upon completion of the curriculum. The total picture must then be broken down so that sequential competencies can be assigned to each essential course in order for students to master competencies. The competencies expected for each course are then stated in the syllabus as observable or measurable student outcomes. The objectives are essential so students can be apprized of the instructor's expectations.

Assigned Readings. The educational process is stronger when students are required to seek information for themselves through reading. The nature and sources of the reading may vary. Not only can the library provide excellent resources, but the Internet can also be a source of reading material.

Description of Instructional Procedures. Students who prepare thoroughly for class will alter their preparation to match the instructional procedures selected by the instructor. Although the lecture is the most popular method, it is also the least effective if used alone. Other methods include the Socratic Method, seminars, group activities, problem solving/case study sessions, cooperative learning, and laboratory experiences.

Course Requirements. This section of a syllabus should inform students of examinations, papers, presentations, projects, academic policies, and evaluation criteria and calculations. Including specific descriptions of the criteria for earning each grade facilitates the development of self-evaluation in students.

Conclusion. Many of the problems that teachers experience are a direct result of poorly constructed syllabi. The construction of a good syllabus requires a comprehensive knowledge of the discipline and time to carefully plan a structure that is based on the teacher's knowledge of student's needs and learning styles. Students' successes are the pride of every teacher. Take the time to plan and reap great rewards.

PURPOSE SETTING QUESTIONS

1. Write the purpose of a course syllabus.
2. List the relevant information that should be included in a course syllabus.
3. Describe the way course objectives should be stated.
4. Explain the rationale for the list of required text(s) and readings for the course.
5. Justify the necessity for the employment of a variety of instructional methods.

6. Integrate descriptions of three instructional procedures into an existing course or proposed syllabus.

7. Rank the aforementioned instructional procedures in terms of their effectiveness from most effective to least effective.

8. Match the course requirement to the relevant course objectives.

9. Name the administrative document that gives course policies.

10. Translate what each letter grade represents to a numerical grade.

VOCABULARY

TECHNICAL TERMS	COMMON TERMS
Cognitive Levels	Intellectual Ranks
Table of Specifications	Test Blueprint
Mission	Purpose
Goal	Long-Range Ambition
Objective	Observable, Measurable Intention
Learning Outcome	Measurable Result
Cooperative Learning	Joint Scholarship
Test	Sample Behavior
Term Paper	Scholarly Document
Project	Supplemental task
Presentation	Conveyed Information
Socratic Questioning	Systematically seeking truth
Interview	Qualification Evaluation
Assessment	Quantitative Measurement
Evaluation	Qualitative Measurement

SPECIAL PROJECT

(Out-of-Class Activity)

Critique the sample syllabus entitled "Reflective Teaching in Biology." Compare the sample syllabus to the guidelines to determine if the sample contains all of the required parts. Evaluate the effectiveness and adequacy of each part represented.

Motivational and Creative Activity

Plan a syllabus using this outline as a guide.

WRITING A COURSE SYLLABUS

A Step-by-Step Outline

A syllabus should include the following information:

A. Core Concept of the Course

B. Relevant information about the Course

1. Course number, title, section, meeting days and times, and location
2. Course description
3. Credit awarded for course
4. Statement of prerequisites
5. Intended audience
6. Instructor's name, office location, office hours, office telephone number, electronic mail address, and fax number

C. Course Objectives--stated in terms of observable and/or measurable student outcomes

D. Readings

1. Required text(s)
2. Supplementary readings

E. Description of Instructional Procedures

  1. Lecture

  2. Socratic questioning

  3. Seminar

  4. Group activities

  5. Problem-solving sessions/case studies

  6. Cooperative learning

  7. Laboratory experiences

F. Course Requirements

  1. Academic

    a. Tests

    b. Term papers

    c. Projects

    d. Presentations

    e. Grading criteria

    f. Course policy

    g. Course schedule

  2. Administrative

    a. Policy regarding "I" and "W" grades

    b. Policy regarding academic history

    c. Policy regarding class attendance

    d. Policy regarding missing or late assignments

  3. Evaluation of students

    a. Specific assignments or requirements used to evaluate each objective and criteria for scoring or scaling these procedures

    b. Specific objectives used to construct test items

c. Specific formula used for translating scores into grades

d. Quantity of testing emphasis used to reflect teaching emphasis

e. Point value of item used to reflect teaching emphasis

f. Table of specifications to justify relevance of test items to course objectives.

SOUTHERN UNIVERSITY

COURSE SYLLABUS

(SAMPLE)

REFLECTIVE TEACHING IN BIOLOGY

WELCOME!

<u>Core Concept</u>. The ultimate purpose of this course is to simultaneously totally immerse prospective biology teachers in theory and practice of teaching biology. The readings were selected with a comprehensive view of what is expected to occur in an effectively taught biology class. The laboratory activities were designed to afford students an opportunity to practice the theories learned from the readings. This integrated approach to teacher preparation produces stronger teachers than traditional practices produced.

Course Number EDCI 423 Section I

10:00 A.M. Monday, Wednesday and Friday -- Room 295 Stewart Hall.

Catalog Description: The purpose of this course is to allow biology teachers to analyze leading biological concepts and to design and/or to select innovative pedagogies for classroom and laboratory instruction. This course is intended for secondary education majors.

Course credit: 4 hours.

FALL SEMESTER 2000

INSTRUCTOR: Dr. B. Goode

OFFICE (Tentative):   Stewart Hall, Room 110

Monday: 11-12 & 1-2

Tuesday: 3-4

Thursday: 2-4

Note: Other times may be arranged by appointment

TELEPHONE/FAX: (504) 771-0000   **E-MAIL:** 1-800-771-ABCD

Specific Objectives:

1. Prepare to work with students by focusing on major biological concepts.

2. Establish the foundation for building professional knowledge about biology.

3. Examine ways for using professional knowledge to make sound biological teaching decisions.

4. Integrate selected educational theory and relevant research with actual day-to-day teaching practice.

5. Synthesize the reflective, school-based, journal writing of concurrent teaching internship with selected metacognitive strategies designed to promote reflection about biological content.

6. Analyze excerpts of a major biology educational reform document.

7. Use conceptual framework for content-related decision making in biological teaching.

Instructional Procedures

* Socratic Questioning
* Problem-solving sessions
* Cooperative learning
* Laboratory

REQUIRED COURSE TEXTS

COLLEGE BIOLOGY INSTRUCTION: AN INTERDISCIPLINARY APPROACH. (Copyright 1988). Marcus Roy, Fan Wang and William Ford. Burlington, MA: Times. CIAIA.

GENERAL BIOLOGY. (Copyright 1993). A. Mader. Burlington, MA: Times. GBT.

COLLEGE BIOLOGY LAB MANUAL. (Copyright 1993). Southern University Biology Faculty. Dubuque, IA: William C. Brown. CBL.

SUPPLEMENTAL EXCERPTS

BIOLOGY FOR ALL AMERICANS. (Copyright 1995). American Association for the Advancement of Biology: Washington, DC. (No Purchase-Excerpts provided by the instructor).

COURSE SCHEDULE
Reading Schedule and Course Evaluation Schedule
August 25 - Monday - Read - CIAIA   HOMEWORK Chapter
DISCIPLINE Chapter

August 27 - Wednesday - Complete - CIAIA   Discipline in Your Classroom
Modes of Instruction

August 29 - Friday - Read - CIAIA   Quiz #1 on New Content
SENT AWAY Chapter
RECOVERY

September 2 - Monday - Complete - CIAIA   Feedback
The Structure of Biology

September 4 - Wednesday - Read - CIAIA   Quiz #2 on New Content
THE SCIENCE FAIR

September 6 - Friday - Read - CBL, GBT "Biology Everyday World Interface"

September 9 - Monday - Read - CIAIA	Quiz #3 on New Content
September 11 - Wednesday - Read - GBT	"Biology Everyday World Interface"
September 13-Friday-Read-CIAIA; GBT	"Design of Instructional Strategies"
September 16-Monday-Complete-CIAIA	Quiz #4 on New Content Evaluation of Instruction
September 18-Wednesday-CBL	Review for Examination Read "Resources of Biological Instruction"
September 20-Friday	Mid-Term
September 23-Monday	Review of Examination
September 26-November 25	Field Assignments Read "Biological Learning for the Future"* (Observations, Teaching)
November 27 - 29	Thanksgiving Holidays

Beyond this point in the course, the emphasis is on reading brief excerpts from and then implementing **Biology for All Americans**, in addition to putting into practice what we have studied. Assignments will be given orally on a weekly basis.

---

*Excerpts from BIOLOGY FOR ALL AMERICANS

COURSE FINAL EXAMINATION: To be scheduled by the University. It will involve reflective writing on ten course topics to be announced before the exam and unique answers are expected.

ACADEMIC AND ADMINISTRATIVE POLICIES

COURSE GRADING SCHEME

What Each Grade Represents

The Grade of F

Here are the typical characteristics of the work of a student who receives an F. A close examination reveals:

The student does not understand basic principles of education, instructional strategies, or student learning. He is unable to analyze what he observes in someone else's classroom or his own, does not justify his selection of instructional procedures, and offers no suggestions for improvement. The writing reflects poor grammar, organization, and a lack of continuity of his teaching. Ideas are not clearly and precisely articulated.

The Grade of D

D-level work demonstrates only a minimum level of understanding of the basic principles of educational instructional strategies, or student learning. The student superficially analyzes classroom activities, can only partially justify his selection of instructional procedures, and makes ineffective suggestions for improving his teaching. The writing only occasionally reflects educated usage. Ideas are vaguely articulated.

The Grade of C

C-level work reflects the initial stage of understanding of the basic principles of education, instructional strategies, and student learning. The student's analysis of classroom activities is often accurate, though sometimes inaccurate. Most of the selected instructional procedures are appropriate and justifiable. The suggestions for improving his teaching are generally good. Usually, the writing reflects educated usage, and the ideas are clearly articulated.

The Grade of B

B-level work reflects an understanding of the basic principles of education, instructional strategies, and student learning and their relationship to the teaching of content. He usually selects appropriate instructional procedures and is able to justify most of them. The writing reflects educated usage, is logically organized, identifies competing points of view, and is usually clearly and precisely articulated.

The Grade of A

A-level work reflects a clear understanding of basic educational principles, instructional strategies, and student learning and their relationship to the teaching of biology. The student is able to analyze activities in any classroom; he selects appropriate and justifiable instructional procedures; and he develops alternatives for improvement of his teaching. His writing reflects educated usage, is logically organized, identifies competing points of view and is clearly and precisely articulated.

Quality of Participation in Class Discussions, Reading Assignments, and Learning Activities 1/4

Four Quizzes 1/4

October 6th Design of Instructional Strategies and Field Assignment Reports1/4

Mid-Term/Final Examination 1/4

Attendance

The educational quality of a small class, such as this one, is critically dependent on the presence and participation of each class member. Your punctual and consistent course attendance is not only part of your participation grade, but also an important indicator that faculty members use in evaluating your work habits when writing a letter of recommendation for you. We will start on time, and trust you will be among us. In case of illness or emergency, please leave a message on my office answering machine telling me of your impending absence.

Missing Or Late Assignments

It is the responsibility of the student to contact/interview classmates to find out what was taught and what was assigned at any class session that he/she missed. For University-excused absences, the missing work is then due one class session beyond the student's return to this class.

Policies Regarding I/W Grades And Academic Honesty

The University's policies are clearly stated in the current catalog. The instructor totally supports all academic and administrative catalog policies.

Student Comments And Suggestions

The instructor welcomes student comments and suggestions intended to improve the course. They may be offered at the end of any class session. Appointments to meet with the instructor can also be scheduled then.

RESOURCE PLACES IN THE COMMUNITY

John B. Cade Library
Southern University
Baton Rouge, LA   (504) 771-4990

Writing Center
Southern University
Baton Rouge, LA   (504) 771-2503

CHAPTER 14

HELPING STUDENTS USE BACKGROUND EXPERIENCES TO GET ALL "FIRED UP"

By: Emma Thomas Pitts

INTRODUCTION

Getting students interested in classroom work in the Twentieth Century is a full-time job in itself. The classroom teacher has to compete with the outside world; i.e., drugs, television, teenage pregnancies, single parenting, extended families, violence in and out of the schools, just to name a few.

America is known as the "melting pot." Cultural diversity is a hot topic today because of the varied backgrounds. Backgrounds include the children of minority groups such as Vietnamese-American, African-American, Hispanic-American, and Native-American students, persons from low socioeconomic backgrounds, the homeless, and many persons who speak English as a second language (Flores, Cousin, and Diaz, 1991). Further, social unrest, changes in family structure, and tensions within communities also contribute to the differences in the American classrooms. With the passage of Public School Law 94-142, an increasing number of students who are developmentally delayed are being mainstreamed into regular classrooms.

Since cultural diversity is a major part of today's classrooms, there are some specific ways that the teacher can make background experiences a plus instead of a minus.

"Open Dialogue Day" is a time set aside (preferably each Friday of the week with a different culture represented) just for students to exchange information about their respective backgrounds. Students are encouraged to wear native apparel, bring samples of food, literature, and retell stories about themselves and families in an open forum. Even the most inhibited student will become "fired up" as he relives the past of his ancestors. Other students will become equally motivated because they will share in the enthusiasm of the "storytellers" and become knowledgeable about other cultures.

Using newspapers to find articles on topics discussed and substituting vocabulary used in the articles with those of individual cultures is another effective method of keeping students in close contact with their heritage and allowing them the freedom to be who they are.

Creating bulletin boards displaying aspects of cultures that will represent the topic under discussion will serve as a visual display, as well as a constant reminder of blending cultural experiences with that of printed textbook data. Students will forever be reminded that what goes on in the classroom should and will be applicable to situations outside of the classroom.

It is a must in our society that individual differences be respected and encouraged in sound educational programs. Students must be made aware that everybody has something to offer and that all learning is not limited to textbook study only. In fact, using background experiences enhances and makes the words printed in a textbook "come alive."

VOC

TECHNICAL TERMS	
Culture	
Legacy	
Chronicle	
Concept	
Experience	
Display	S..ow
Explore	Search
Visual Aid	Newspaper
Expound	State
Encourage	Inspire
Topic	Subject
Inquiry	Question
Diverse	Different
Association	Relationship
Schemata	Background Experiences

PURPOSE SETTING QUESTIONS

1. What is education?
2. How can background experiences be integrated with textbook information?
3. Why is experience of paramount importance in classroom discussions?
4. What can classroom teachers do to motivate students?
5. How can cultures learn from other cultures?

6. What is interculturation?

7. What are mores?

8. What are customs?

9. How can teachers compete in a positive way with the outside world?

10. How can background experiences enhance learning?

SPECIAL PROJECTS
(Out-of-Class Activities)

1. Develop a bibliography of trade books that can be exchanged with classmates to promote understanding of different cultures.

2. Develop a program highlighting diversity and invite entire student body.

3. Write an advertisement for an item or service that could be used in a newspaper or magazine.

4. Visit various neighborhoods and discuss findings with class.

Motivational And Creative Activities

1. Open Dialogue Day

   Students will share information concerning respective cultures in an open forum each Friday of the week.

2. Guest Speakers

   Students will invite members of their respective families to share ancestral backgrounds with class.

3. Displays

   Students will secure artifacts from family members for display in the classroom.

4. Language Experience Approach

   Students will select an object from another culture and write a poem, story, drama, or lyrics to a song about it.

5. Partnership Grouping

Students will choose a peer in the classroom. The peer will learn as much information as possible about his/her "partner" and share findings with the class.

RESOURCE PLACES IN THE COMMUNITY

1. Individual Students' Homes

2. Places of Worship (Examples: Greater King David Baptist Church, Jewish Synagogues, Mosques)

3. State, Local, and School Libraries (Such as Goodwood Library, Baton Rouge, LA)

4. Heritage Tours (Such as Louisiana African American Odyssey, Inc., Tours Specializing in African American History, Baton Rouge, LA)

BIBLIOGRAPHY

Abrams, D. (1986). Lymphadenopathy syndrome in male homosexuals. New York: Raven Press, pp. 75-82.

Alderman, Janice. (1990). Facts about AIDS. New York: Little, Brown and Company.

Allman, Dennis. (1986). AIDS in the minds of America. New York: Anchor Press, pp. 108-169.

Allman, W. R. (1986). Tracking AIDS to the ends of the earth. Esquire, December 1986, pp. 211-212.

Altman, Howard B., Cashino, William E. (1992). Idea paper. Writing a Syllabus. Kansas: Manhattan, Center for Faculty Evaluation and Development (27).

Aptheker, Herbert. (1968). A documentary history of the negro people in the United States. Vol. 1 of 3 vols. New York.

Ardley, Neil. (1984). Discovering electricity. New York: Franklin Watts.

Ardley, Neil. (1984). Making things move. New York: Franklin Watts.

Avery, Carol. (1992). Guide students' choices: Ready to write. Instructor; v102, nr, p 32, Nov - Dec.

Banks, J.A. (1979). Teaching strategies for ethnic studies. Boston: Allyn & Bacon.

Basler, Roy P. (1953). The collected work of Abraham Lincoln. 8 vols. New Brunswick, New Jersey.

Beale, Howard K. (1960). Diary of Gideon Welles. Secretary of the Navy under Lincoln and Johnson. Vol III of 3 vols. New York.

Bell, Howard Holman. (1964). Minutes of the proceedings of the national negro conventions 1830-1864. New York.

Belman, A. (1988). Brian function declines in children with AIDS. Cambridge: Harvard University Press.

Benza, Joseph. (1987). Preventing AIDS. Cincinnati: JALSCO Publishing Company, Inc.

Berger, Melvin. (1983). Energy. New York: Franklin Watts.

Berlin, Ira, et al., eds. (1983). Freedom: A documentary history of emancipation. 1861-1867. Series 2. The black military experience. New York.

Biggar, R. Antibody variation in AIDS and AIDS risk: Homosexual men. New York: The New Journal of Medicine 313: 1498-1505.

Biggar, R. (1986). The AIDS problem in Africa. Los Angeles: Bard Publishing Company, 1986.

Blassingame, John W. (1972). The slave community: Plantation life in the antebellum south. Oxford University Press.

Blassingame, John W. ed (1982). The Frederick Douglass papers. Series I Speeches, Debates, and Interviews. Vols. I and III of 3 vols to date. New Haven: 1979.

Blassingame, John W, Henderson, Mae G., Dunn, Jessica M. eds. (1981). Antislavery newspaper and periodicals: Annotated index of letters, 1817-1871. Vol III, 1836-1864 of 5 vols. New York.

Bloom, Benjamin et.al (1971). Handbook on formative and summative evaluation of student learning. New York: New York, McGraw-Hill.

Bowen, D. (1987). Immunopathogensis of the acquired immunodeficiency syndrome science 439: 352-367.

Branley, Franklyn M. (1986). Gravity is a mystery. New York: Crowell.

Breen, Maxine. (1988). AIDS: An acquired community problem. New York: Canterbury Press.

Brisk, Maria Estela. (1991). Toward multilingual and multicultural mainstream education. Journal of education, Spring, v173 n2 p 114(16).

Brotz, Howard, ed. (1971). The negro in the rebellion. 1867; rpr. New York.

Brown, William. (1857). American slavery and colour. New York.

Brownlee, Shannon. "Refurbishing the body." U.S. nes and work report. Nov 12, 1990, v109 n19 p76(3).

Cameron, Derek. (1978). Hi-fi stereo installation simplified. Reston, Virginia: Reston Publishing Company, Inc. A Prentice-Hall Company.

Cantwell, Alan. (1987). AIDS the mystery and the solution. Cambridge: The England Press.

Chapman, Phillip. (1976). Young scientist book of electricity. Tulsa, OK: EDC.

Cipra, Cipra. (1990). Big number breakdown. Science. July 29, 1990, v248, N4963, p. 1608 (1).

City Utilities: (1986). Our basic services. Van Nup, Ca: Aims Media, 16 min color 16 mm film and videocassette.

Codianni, A.V. (1981). Toward educational equality for all: A planning guide for integrating multicultural nonsexist education into the K-12 curriculum. Manhattan, Kansas: Midwest Race and Sex Desegregation Centers.

Cofflin, Haase. (1989). Human immuno-deficiency virus. Science 232:697-705.

Cortes, C., Metcalf, F., and Hawke, S. (1976). Understanding you and them tips for teaching about ethnicity. Boulder, Colorado: Social Science Education Consortium.

Coutler, Merton, (195). The confederate states of America 1861-1865.

Curran, Morgan. (1991). The epidemiology of AIDS: Journal of American Medical Association. 229:1352-1359.

Daley, Janet. Sinister ways of classroom cheats. Times educational supplement. July 26, 1991 n3917 p 15(1).

Delany, Martin R. (1968). The condition, elevation, emigration, and destiny of colored people of the United States. 1852 rpr. New York.

Donald, David, ed. (1954). Inside Lincoln's cabinet: The Civil War Diaries of Salmon. P. Chase. New York.

Douglass, Frederick. (1881). The life and times of Frederick Douglass. Written by himself. rpr. New York: 2962.

DuBois, W.E.B. (1969). The souls of black folk. 1903; rpr. New York.

Duvall, H. (1987). Aids Strike black children at high rate. New York: The Whitson Publishing Company.

Energy Savers. (1982). Kansas City, MO: Walk Disney, 9-min color 16mm film.

Farer, Frances. (1993). Thing on your feet. Times educational supplement, Oct 29, n4035 pf10(1).

Fischetti, Mark. Gas vaccine: Bioengineered immunization could shield against nerve gas. Scientific American. April 1991, v264 n4 p153(2).

Fitter, Anne. (1986). The truth about AIDS. New York: Bard Publishing Co.

Flores, B., Cousin, P.T., and Diaz, E. (1991). Transforming deficit myths about learning, language and culture. Language Arts 68: 369-379.

Foner, Phillip S. (1950). The life and writings of Frederick Douglass. 5 vols., New York.

Freeman, John and Hallings, Martin. (1983). Mechanics. Morristown, NJ: Silver Burdett.

Garnet, Henry Highland. (1969). An address to the slaves of the United States of America. 1848; rpr. New York.

Gollnick, Donna M. (1983). Multicultural education in a pluralistic society. St. Louis, Missouri: The C.V. Mosby Company.

Goodell, William. (1844). Slavery and antislavery. 1852; rpr. New York: 1968. Views of American Constitutional Law in its Bearing Upon American Slavery, N.P.

Grady, Dorothy. (1990). Education and AIDS. Barkley: University California Press.

Grant, C.A. (1977). Multicultural education: Commitments, issues and applications. Washington, DC: Association for Supervision and Curriculum Development.

Grant, C.A. (1977). In praise of diversity: Multicultural classroom applications. Omaha: University of Omaha.

Green, Septina. (1991). Class-to-class writing projects: First graders and fourth graders team up. Learning: v19 n7 pp 54-56, March.

Griffiths, Julia, ed (1854). Autographs for freedom. 2 vols. Rochester, NY.

Guttentag, M., Bray H. (1976). Undoing sex stereotypes: Research and resources for educators. New York: McGraw-Hill.

Hansen-Krening, N. (1979). Competence and creativity in language arts: A multiethnic focus. Reading, Mass.: Addison-Wesley.

Hausherr, Rosmarie. (1990). Children and the AIDS virus. New York: Houghton Mifflin Company.

Heller, Carol. (1992). Within worlds: Students share culture through writing. Teaching Tolerance: v1 n2 pp 36-43 Fall.

Henbest, Nigel, Cooper, Heather. 91983). Physics. New York: Franklin Watts.

Henslee, T., Jones, P. (1977). Freedom of reach for young children: Nonsexist early childhood education. Washington, DC, Office of Education.
Higginson, Thomas Wentworth. (1969). Army life in a black regiment. New York.

Jampole, Ellen S. (1994). Academically gifted students' use of imagery for creative writing. Journal of creative behavior; v 28 n1 pp 1-15.

Johnson, L. O. (1974). Nonsexist curricular materials for elementary schools. Old Westbury, N.Y.: Feminist Press.

Johnson, Earvin "Magic". (1992). What you can do to avoid AIDS. New York: Random House.

Jonsen, Cooke. (1986). AIDS and ethic. Issues in Science and technology. pp.56-65.

Kant, S. (1985). The transmission of HTLV-III, JAMA, April.

Kent, Amanda, Ward, Alan. (1983). Physics. Tulsa: EDC.

Kettle Kamp, Larry. (1982). The magic of sound. New York: Morrow.

King, E.W. (1980). Teaching ethnic awareness: Method and materials for the elementary schools. Santa Monica, California. Goodyear.

Laithwaite, Eric. (1986). Force: The power behind movement. New York: Franklin Watts.

Landesman, Ginny. (1985). The AIDS epidemic. New England: New England Journal of Medicine, 521.

Lane, Michael S., Mansour, Ali H., Harpell, John L. Operations Research techniques: A longitudinal upgrade. Interfaces. March-April, 1993, v23 n2 p 63(6).

Levenson, Elaine. (1985). Teaching children about science. Englewood Cliffs, NJ: Prentice-Hall.

Lewis, Aaron, Lieberman, Klony. Near-field optical imaging with a non-evanescently excited high brightness light course of sub-wavelength dimensions. Nature. Nov 21, 1991, v 354, n6350, p 21493).

Marsh, Luther R. (1855). ed. Writings and speeches of Alvan Stewart on slavery, New York: 1860. Proceedings of the Radical Abolition Convention. June 26-28, 1855. New York.

Matthews, Neslund. (1989). The initial impact of AIDS on public health. Journal of the American Medical Association. 257:344-352.

McIntosh, Margaret E. (1989). Idea Exchange: Poems to get children writing. Writing Teacher; v2 n5 pp 41-43 April-May.

McKeachie, W.J. (1981). Teaching tips: A guidebook for the beginning college teacher. Developing a course syllabus. Mass: Lexington, D.C. Health.

McLoughlin, William G ed (1968). The American evangelicals. 1800-1900. An anthology. New York.

McNeil, E., Allen, J., Schmidt, J. (1975). Cultural awareness for young children. The Learning Tree.

McNeil, Mary Jean (1975). How things begin. Tulsa, OK: EDC.

McPherson, James M ed (1965). The negro civil war: How American negroes felt and acted during the war for the union. New York.

Mitgutsch, Ali. (1985). From Swamp to coal. Minneapolis: Carolhoda.

Pasternak, M.G. (1977) Helping kids learn multi-cultural concepts: A handbook of strategies. Nashville, Tennessee: Nashville Consortium Teacher Corporation.

Paul, Richard. (1994). Critical thinking workshops. The logical structural design. Rohnert Park: CA. Center for Critical thinking.

Peterson, Rita et al (1984). Science and society: A sourcebook for elementary and junior high school teachers. Columbus, OH: Merrill.

Quisenberry, James D. Linguistic and cultural differences teachers should know. Childhood education. Winter 1993, v70 n2 p96K(1).

Redpath, James. (1860). Echoes of harpers ferry. 1860: rpr. New York: 1969 ed. A guide to Hayi. Boston.

Rheingold, Howard. (1992). At the beginning of the twentieth Century. Whole earth review. Fall, n76 pCOV(2).

Richardson, James D. (1897). A compilation of the messages and paper of the Presidents, 1789-1897. Vol VI of 10 vols., Washington, D.C.

Ruchames, Louis, ed 91976). The letter of William Lloyd Garrison. Vol. IV of 4 vols. Cambridge, Mass.

Russell, Colin. The right accent. Times educational supplement. Nov. 8, 1991 n3932 pS10(1).

Schrier, Eric W., Allman, William F. (1984).Newton at the bat. New York: Scribber.

Selsam, Millicent. Up, Down and Around: The Force of Gravity.

Singleton, Loy A. (1983). Telecommunications in the information age. Cambridge, Massachusetts: Ballinger Publishing Company.

Smith, Bernice, Taylor, Lelia H. (1993). Testing development paradigm. Baton Rouge, Louisiana, Cognitive Skills Development Program at Southern University.

Speech, Language and hearing: Normal processes and disorders. (1978). Reading, Massachusetts: Addison-Wesley Publishing Company.

Spooner, Lysander. (1965). The unconstitutionality of slavery. 2nd ed. 1845; rpr. New York.

Sprague, Rosette Douglas. (1900). My mother as I recall. Washington, D.C.: Library of Congress, Microfilm.

Stevens, S.S., Warshofsky, Fred (1990). and editors of Life, sound and hearing. New York: Time Incorporated.

Stiffe, John. (1990). AIDS in the black community. New York: Holt-Rinehart. Winston Publishing Company.

Stoning, Herbert, ed. (1972). The ideological origins of black nationalism. Boston.

Strongin, Herb. (1976). Science on a shoestring. Menlo Park, CA: Addison-Wesley.

Stuckey, Sterling, ed. (1972). The black nationalism. New York.

Tice, Terrance N. Classroom metaphors. Times educational supplement. Nov. 8, 1991 n3932 pS10(1).

Tocqueville, Alexis de (1981). Democracy in America. Edited by Thomas Bender. New York.

Walker, David. (1969). Walker's appeal in four articles. 1830; rpr. New York.

Ward, Samuel Ringgold. (1968). Autobiography of a fugitive negro. 1855; rpr. New York.

Washington, Booker T. (1965). Up from slavery. 1903; rpr. New York.

Welles, Gideon. (1911). Diary of Gideon Welles. edited by John T. Morse, 3 vols. Boston.

Whyman, Kathyrn. (1986). Forces in Action, from Science today Series. New York: Gloucester.

Williams, General Thomas. (1868). Letters of General Thomas Williams. 1862. Boston.

Zubrowski, Bernie. (1986). Wheels at Work: Building and Experimenting with Models of Machines. New York: Morrow.

MELLEN STUDIES IN EDUCATION